Canadian Living's Best

Breads & Pizzas

B Y

Elizabeth Baird

A N D

The Food Writers of Canadian Living® Magazine
and The Canadian Living Test Kitchen

A MADISON PRESS BOOK

PRODUCED FOR

BALLANTINE BOOKS AND CANADIAN LIVING

Ballantine Books
A Division of
Random House of
Canada Limited
2775 Matheson Blvd East
Mississauga, Ontario
Canada
L4W 4P7

Canadian Living
Telemedia
Communications Inc.
25 Sheppard Avenue West
Suite 100
North York, Ontario
Canada
M2N 6S7

Canadian Cataloguing in Publication Data

Baird, Elizabeth
Breads & pizzas

(Canadian living's best)
"A Madison Press book."
Includes index.
ISBN 0-345-39868-8

1. Bread. 2. Pizza. I. Title. II. Series.

TX769.B26 1998   641.8'15   C97-932640-0

EDITORIAL DIRECTOR: Hugh Brewster
PROJECT EDITOR: Wanda Nowakowska
EDITORIAL ASSISTANCE: Beverley Renahan, Rosemary Hillary
PRODUCTION DIRECTOR: Susan Barrable
PRODUCTION COORDINATOR: Donna Chong
BOOK DESIGN AND LAYOUT: Gordon Sibley Design Inc.
COLOR SEPARATION: Colour Technologies
PRINTING AND BINDING: Friesen Corporation

CANADIAN LIVING ADVISORY BOARD: Elizabeth Baird, Bonnie Baker Cowan,
Anna Hobbs, Caren King

CANADIAN LIVING'S BEST BREADS & PIZZAS
was produced by Madison Press Books
which is under the direction of Albert E. Cummings

Madison Press Books
40 Madison Avenue
Toronto, Ontario, Canada
M5R 2S1

Printed in Canada

Contents

Panettone (p. 26)

Wheat Tortillas (p. 58)

Introduction

Breads and pizzas — why make them in this day and age? Supermarket shelves are stacked with loaves of all kinds, and a simple phone call brings a crusty, gooey pizza to your door within the half hour.

Good question — for which there are good answers. For starters, there's the irresistible, come-hither aroma of freshly baked bread. With a loaf hot from the oven, it doesn't take long for the family to gather in the kitchen, ready for the it's-cool-enough-now signal to slice and slather.

Homemade bread also invites you to make choices — healthy whole wheat, the variety of dark rye, chewy oats and a whole cupboard full of seeds, nuts, fruit, spices and herbs. Soft crust, crusty, shiny or chewy? Dense soft crumb? Or a loose and holey sourdough? Take your pick from among glossy sandwich loaves, homey cross-hatched rustic breads, flour-veiled freeform rounds, rich festive braids, pans of dinner buns, flatbread from around the world, and much more.

Most of all, good bread is about taste, as are other members of the bread family — focaccia, calzone and pizza. You can make better-tasting bread for less money than store-bought, and superior homemade pizza is definitely a bargain compared to delivered.

But bread making takes time, you argue. And the process is complicated, the results uncertain. It's true that making bread *does* take time, but after the first knead, all dough requires is an occasional check, then shaping. In between, you can tend to other pleasures and pursuits. There's no magic to kneading — it's just pushing and folding the dough around until it's stretchy and smooth. And if you aren't sure, the food processor, dough hook on the mixer, or the bread machine is there to help. Afraid the yeast won't work? Just respect the best-before date. And flours made from Canadian wheat set the standard worldwide and ensure results.

Bread making is relaxing, not only because you enjoy the opportunity to punch, pound and pummel, but also because bread dough is forgiving. If it's too wet? Add a little more flour. And, if you have to leave just when the bread is rising in a cozy spot, transfer it to the fridge to slow down the process, or punch it down and give yourself an extra hour until it's convenient to put the loaf into the oven.

No need to say more. Let the easy-to-follow, guaranteed-to-please recipes in *Canadian Living's Best Breads & Pizzas* be your invitation — either to lay the foundation for your bread making or to expand and rev up your repertoire to include dozens of delicious new breads for all occasions and tastes.

Elizabeth Baird

(Front) Italian Rustic Loaf (p. 14); Sourdough Bread (p. 21)

Best of the Basics

Lay the foundation for a future of successful bread making with this selection of classic loaves — starting with a crusty white that illustrates basic kneading, rising and shaping techniques, then on to rye, sourdough, whole wheat, oats, seeds and even potatoes as the basis for outstanding breads.

Really Good Basic Bread ▶

There's no better way to start out as a baker of bread than with this comprehensive, step-by-step recipe. Results — and satisfaction — are guaranteed. The hardest part will be keeping bread admirers at bay when the crusty, golden loaves come out of the oven.

Per slice: about
- 120 calories
- 2 g fat
- 3 g protein
- 22 g carbohydrate

1 tsp	granulated sugar	5 mL
1 cup	warm water	250 mL
1	pkg active dry yeast (or 1 tbsp/15 mL)	1
1 cup	milk	250 mL
2 tbsp	granulated sugar	25 mL
2 tbsp	butter	25 mL
1-1/2 tsp	salt	7 mL
5 cups	(approx) all-purpose flour	1.25 L
1	egg yolk	1
1 tbsp	water	15 mL

● In large bowl, dissolve 1 tsp (5 mL) sugar in warm water. Sprinkle in yeast; let stand for 10 minutes or until frothy.

● Meanwhile, in saucepan, heat together milk, 2 tbsp (25 mL) sugar, butter and salt over low heat just until butter is melted; let cool to lukewarm. Add to yeast mixture.

● With electric mixer, gradually beat in 3 cups (750 mL) of the flour until smooth, about 3 minutes. With wooden spoon, gradually stir in enough of the remaining flour to make stiff dough. Turn out dough onto lightly floured surface. Knead for 10 minutes or until smooth and elastic. Place in greased bowl, turning to grease all over. Cover with plastic wrap; let rise in warm draft-free place until doubled in bulk, 1 to 1-1/2 hours.

● Punch down dough; turn out onto lightly floured surface. Knead into ball; cover and let rest for 10 minutes. Divide dough in half; shape each into smooth ball.

● Gently pull each ball into 11- x 8-inch (28 x 20 cm) rectangle. Starting at narrow end, roll up into cylinder; pinch along bottom to smooth and seal. Fit into two greased 8- x 4-inch (1.5 L) loaf pans. Cover and let rise until doubled in bulk, about 1 hour.

● Whisk egg yolk with water; brush over loaves. Bake in center of 400°F (200°C) oven for about 30 minutes or until golden brown and loaves sound hollow when tapped on bottom. Remove from pans; let cool on racks. Makes 2 loaves, 12 slices each.

BREAD MACHINE METHOD

● Into pan of machine, add (in order) 1/2 cup (125 mL) each water and milk, 1 tbsp (15 mL) each granulated sugar and cubed butter, 1/2 tsp (2 mL) salt, 3 cups (750 mL) all-purpose flour and 1-1/4 tsp (6 mL) quick-rising (instant) dry yeast. (Do not let yeast touch liquid.) Choose basic setting or regular/light. Let baked loaf cool on rack. Makes 1 loaf.

French Baguette ◄

1 tsp	granulated sugar	5 mL
2-1/2 cups	warm water	625 mL
1	pkg active dry yeast (or 1 tbsp/15 mL)	1
5-1/2 cups	(approx) all-purpose flour	1.25 L
1/4 cup	skim milk powder	50 mL
1 tbsp	salt	15 mL
	Cornmeal	

● In large bowl, dissolve sugar in warm water. Sprinkle in yeast; let stand for 10 minutes or until frothy. With electric mixer, gradually beat in 3 cups (750 mL) of the flour, skim milk powder and salt, beating for about 3 minutes or until smooth. With wooden spoon, gradually stir in enough of the remaining flour to make stiff dough.

● Turn out dough onto lightly floured surface. Knead for 10 minutes or until smooth and elastic. Place in greased bowl, turning to grease all over. Cover with plastic wrap; let rise in warm draft-free place until almost tripled in bulk, 2 to 2-1/2 hours.

● Punch down dough; cover and let rise until doubled in bulk, 1 to 1-1/2 hours. Grease 2 large heavy baking sheets and dust with cornmeal; set aside.

● Punch down dough; turn out onto lightly floured surface. Knead into smooth ball. Divide dough into quarters; roll each into 14-inch (35 cm) long rope. Place 2 ropes at least 4 inches (10 cm) apart on each prepared baking sheet. Dust tops with flour. Cover and let rise until doubled in bulk, about 1 hour.

● Place inverted baking sheet on middle rack of 425°F (220°C) oven. Place metal cake pan or pie plate on bottom rack. Heat for 15 minutes. Pour 1 cup (250 mL) water into pan. Using serrated knife, cut 3 long diagonal slashes about 1/4 inch (5 mm) deep along top of each baguette. Baking only 2 baguettes at a time, place baking sheet with baguettes on inverted baking sheet; bake for 20 to 25 minutes or until golden brown and loaves sound hollow when tapped on bottom. Let cool on racks. Makes 4 baguettes, 12 slices each.

*P*atsy Jamieson, for five years our test kitchen manager and now food editor of Eating Well Magazine, *is a masterful baker — witness her method of making that French classic, a perfect baguette.*

Per slice: about
- 54 calories
- trace fat
- 2 g protein
- 11 g carbohydrate

TIP: A pan of hot water, placed on the bottom rack of the oven while loaves are baking, guarantees a crisp crust on French bread.

FLOUR FACTS

● Canada produces the finest wheat in the world, with a high protein content. (In fact, Italy imports Canadian durum wheat to make pasta.)

● All-purpose flour is a mixture of 80 percent hard wheat and 20 percent soft wheat. Because our wheat has such a high protein content, we can use all-purpose flour for our loaves and still get fabulous results.

● Whole wheat flour is milled from the entire wheat kernel, including the bran and germ. It has a richer flavor and higher nutritional value than all-purpose flour.

● All-purpose flour is fine for most bread making, but specialty bread flours are also available at supermarkets and at bulk and health food stores. They have a higher gluten content than all-purpose flour, so you may want to increase liquid and shorten your kneading time slightly.

● You may want to add a small amount of gluten flour (1 to 2 tbsp/15 to 25 mL per loaf) to your bread making. It can add structure to breads made with whole wheat flour or that have a lower proportion of wheat flour to other grains such as rye, barley or oats. Kneading times will be reduced slightly.

● Store all flours in airtight containers; store whole grain flour in the refrigerator or freezer to prevent it from going rancid.

A Classic Loaf and Variations ▶

This versatile dough — make it by hand or in the bread machine — bakes into one glorious loaf or a whole breadbasket of sticks, twists, wreaths and shapes for the holidays and all year round.

Per slice: about
- 135 calories
- 4 g protein
- 2 g fat
- 25 g carbohydrate

TIPS
● For faster rising of bread dough, place bowl of dough over bowl of hot tap water or on top of heating pad set at lowest temperature.
● For best results when baking bread, bake on center rack of preheated oven.

1 tsp	granulated sugar	5 mL
1 cup	warm water	250 mL
2 tsp	active dry yeast	10 mL
1 tbsp	vegetable oil	15 mL
1-1/4 tsp	salt	6 mL
3 cups	(approx) all-purpose flour	750 mL
1	egg yolk	1

● In large bowl, dissolve sugar in warm water. Sprinkle in yeast; let stand for 10 minutes or until frothy. Whisk in oil, salt and 1 cup (250 mL) of the flour. With wooden spoon, gradually beat in enough of the remaining flour to make stiff dough.

● Turn out dough onto lightly floured surface. Knead for about 5 minutes or until smooth and elastic. Place in greased bowl, turning to grease all over. Cover with plastic wrap; let rise in warm draft-free place until doubled in bulk, about 1 hour.

● Punch down dough; turn out onto lightly floured surface. Press into oval shape. Starting at narrow end, roll up into cylinder; pinch along bottom to smooth and seal. Fit into greased 8- x 4-inch (1.5 L) loaf pan. Cover and let rise until doubled in bulk, about 1 hour.

● Brush egg yolk over loaf. Bake in center of 400°F (200°C) oven for about 30 minutes or until golden and loaf sounds hollow when tapped on bottom. Remove from pan; let cool on rack. Makes 1 loaf, 12 slices.

BREAD MACHINE METHOD
● Into pan of machine, add (in order) water, sugar, oil, salt, flour and 1-1/2 tsp (7 mL) quick-rising (instant) dry yeast. (Do not let yeast touch liquid.) Omit egg yolk. Choose basic setting or regular/light setting. Let baked loaf cool on rack. Makes 1 loaf.

VARIATIONS
● PRETZELS: Make dough for Classic Loaf. Let rise as specified; punch down. Divide into 4 portions. Roll out each into 12- x 6-inch (30 x 15 cm) rectangle; cut lengthwise into 6 strips. Shape each into circle, crossing ends over to meet circle at opposite side to form pretzel, pressing to seal; place on lightly greased baking sheet. Brush with egg yolk; sprinkle with 2 tsp (10 mL) coarse salt. Cover lightly with plastic wrap; let rise for 20 minutes. Bake in center of 400°F (200°C) oven for about 15 minutes or until golden and crispy. Makes 24 pretzels.

● BREADSTICKS: Make dough for Classic Loaf. Let rise as specified; punch down. Divide into 4 portions. Roll out each into 12- x 6-inch (30 x 15 cm) rectangle; cut lengthwise into 6 strips. Transfer to lightly greased baking sheet. Brush with egg yolk; sprinkle with 2 tsp (10 mL) coarse salt. Cover lightly with plastic wrap; let rise for 20 minutes. Bake in center of 400°F (200°C) oven for 20 minutes or until golden. Makes 24 breadsticks.

● PARMESAN TWISTS: Make dough for Classic Loaf. Let rise as specified; punch down. Divide in half. Roll out each into 12- x 9-inch (30 x 23 cm) rectangle. Brush each with egg white. Sprinkle 1 rectangle with 1/4 cup (50 mL) freshly grated Parmesan cheese. Place remaining rectangle on top, egg-white side down; press firmly together. Cut lengthwise into 12 strips; twist each to form spiral. Transfer to lightly greased baking sheet. Brush with egg yolk. Cover lightly with plastic wrap; let rise for 20 minutes. Bake in center of 425°F (220°C) oven for about 10 minutes or until golden. Makes 12 twists.

● RED PEPPER PISTACHIO BAGUETTE: Make dough for Classic Loaf. Let rise as specified; punch down. Roll out into 14- x 12-inch (35 x 30 cm) rectangle. Sprinkle with 1/2 cup (125 mL) shelled green pistachios and 1/2 cup (125 mL) chopped sweet red pepper, leaving 1-inch (2.5 cm) border on all sides. Roll up diagonally, pinching edges to seal. Using scissors, make 5 deep cuts crosswise

and evenly spaced across top. If desired, insert a few more nuts and/or red pepper pieces for color. Transfer to lightly greased baking sheet. Brush with egg yolk. Cover lightly with plastic wrap; let rest for 15 minutes. Bake in center of 400°F (200°C) oven for 25 to 30 minutes or until golden. Makes 1 loaf, 32 slices.

● JUMBO POPPY SEED CANDY CANES: Make dough for Classic Loaf. Let rise as specified; punch down. Divide into 6 pieces; roll each into 14-inch (35 cm) length. Brush 3 of the lengths all over with egg yolk; roll in 1/4 cup (50 mL) poppy seeds. Place each poppy seed length beside remaining plain length; gently twist together to form spiral, pinching ends to seal. Transfer to lightly greased baking sheet. Curve one end to form candy cane. Brush plain part of candy cane with egg yolk. Cover lightly with plastic wrap; let rise for 20 minutes. Bake in center of 400°F (200°C) oven for about 12 minutes or until golden. Makes 3 candy canes.

● HOLLY LEAVES: Make dough for Classic Loaf. Let rise as specified; punch down. Roll out into 10-inch (25 cm) circle. With 3-1/2- x 2-inch (9 x 5 cm) holly-shaped cookie cutter, cut out shapes. With sharp knife, cut shallow slash down center to resemble vein of leaf. Transfer to lightly greased baking sheet. Brush with egg yolk; sprinkle each with 1/2 tsp (2 mL) finely chopped green pistachios or other topping, if desired. Cover lightly with plastic wrap; let rise for 20 minutes. Bake in center of 400°F (200°C) oven for 20 minutes or until golden. Makes 16 leaves.

● LARGE WREATHS: Make dough for Classic Loaf. Let rise as specified; punch down. Divide in half; roll out each into 7-inch (18 cm) circle. With two 2-inch (5 cm) round (preferably scalloped) cookie cutters, cut out center of each. Grease cutters well; place in holes in centers. Transfer to lightly greased baking sheet. Brush with egg yolk. Cover lightly with plastic wrap; let rise for 20 minutes. With kitchen scissors, cut about 8 snips horizontally in dough around edge of wreath; place piece of glacé cherry or sweet red pepper in each snip. With cookie cutters still in place, bake in center of 400°F (200°C) oven for 20 minutes or until golden. Remove cutters. (You can bake the centers alongside for a treat for the cook.) Makes 2 large wreaths.

Crusty Crown Loaf ▶

This bread dough is incredibly versatile. The interior is beautifully tender and even, but the crust is crackled and crisp. The six-point slash before baking results in a spectacular crown-shaped loaf. Make it plain, or with any of these delicious Mediterranean add-ins. Or, shape into rolls.

Per slice: about
- 172 calories
- 4 g fat
- 4 g protein
- 21 g carbohydrate

Pinch	granulated sugar	Pinch
3/4 cup	warm water	175 mL
2-1/2 tsp	active dry yeast	12 mL
3/4 cup	milk	175 mL
1/4 cup	olive oil	50 mL
4-3/4 cups	(approx) all-purpose flour	1.175 L
1 tbsp	salt	15 mL
	Cornmeal	

● In large bowl, dissolve sugar in warm water. Sprinkle in yeast; let stand for 10 minutes or until frothy. Stir in milk and oil. Stir in 4-1/2 cups (1.125 L) of the flour and salt to form shaggy, moist dough.

● Turn out dough onto lightly floured surface. Knead for 8 minutes or until smooth and elastic, dusting with as much of the remaining flour as necessary to prevent sticking. Form into ball; place in lightly greased bowl, turning to grease all over. Cover with plastic wrap; let rise in warm draft-free place until doubled in bulk, 1-1/2 to 2 hours.

● Punch down dough; form into ball. Place on cornmeal-dusted baking sheet; cover with damp tea towel and let rise in warm draft-free place until not quite doubled in bulk, 45 to 60 minutes.

● Spray loaf with water. With sharp knife, cut three 1/2-inch (1 cm) deep intersecting slashes across top of loaf. Bake in center of 450°F (230°C) oven for 10 minutes, spraying 3 more times with water. Reduce heat to 400°F (200°C); bake for about 45 minutes longer or until golden brown and loaf sounds hollow when tapped on bottom. Let cool on rack. Makes 1 large loaf, 16 slices.

VARIATIONS

● CRUSTY CROWN SUN-DRIED TOMATO LOAF: Omit oil. Finely chop 1/2 cup (125 mL) oil-packed sun-dried tomatoes. Return to measure; pour in enough oil (either oil from tomatoes or olive oil) to make 1/2 cup (125 mL). Add to water with milk.

● CRUSTY CROWN PESTO LOAF: Omit oil. Add 1/2 cup (125 mL) pesto along with milk.

● CRUSTY CROWN HERB LOAF: Add 1/4 cup (50 mL) chopped fresh rosemary, basil or oregano (or 1 tbsp/15 mL dried) along with milk and oil.

CRUSTY SANDWICH OR DINNER ROLLS

● Make dough as directed for Crusty Crown Loaf or any of its variations through to end of first rise.

● Punch down dough. Divide into 8 pieces for sandwich rolls, 16 pieces for dinner rolls. Form each into ball; place, seam side down, on greased baking sheets. Cover with damp tea towel; let rise in warm draft-free place until not quite doubled in bulk, about 45 minutes. Whisk 1 egg with 1 tbsp (15 mL) water; brush over rolls.

● Bake in center of 400°F (200°C) oven for 20 minutes for dinner rolls, 25 minutes for sandwich rolls, or until golden brown and rolls sound hollow when tapped on bottom. Let cool on rack. Makes 8 sandwich or 16 dinner rolls.

Italian Rustic Loaf

This is the dough that has been emerging from wood-burning ovens and village hearths for centuries. It makes bread with a dark, thick, flour-dusted chewy crust and a porous, moist interior (photo, p. 4). The dough is traditionally very wet and must be kneaded in the bowl, or in a tabletop mixer. But the results are worth the 15 minutes' stickiness. Because you want the air bubbles in the dough to remain there — giving the trademark moist, irregular interior — it is important not to knead the dough or punch it down too vigorously after the first rise.

Per slice: about
- 141 calories
- 2 g fat
- 4 g protein
- 26 g carbohydrate

1-1/2 tsp	granulated sugar	7 mL
2 cups	warm water	500 mL
2 tsp	active dry yeast	10 mL
2 tbsp	olive oil	25 mL
4-1/3 cups	(approx) all-purpose flour	1.075 L
1-1/2 tsp	salt	7 mL

● In large bowl, dissolve sugar in warm water. Sprinkle in yeast; let stand for 10 minutes or until frothy. Stir in oil. Stir in flour and salt to form wet sticky dough.

● Using hands and keeping dough in bowl, begin to work dough. With fingers together, scoop under dough and pull undermost part to top. Give bowl one-quarter turn and scoop again. Repeat turning bowl and scooping dough for 5 minutes. Dough will remain sticky but will feel more elastic.

● Grasping dough with one hand, stretch dough upward out of bowl until it resists stretching; firmly slap dough back into bowl. Continue alternating scooping motion with stretching and slapping for 10 minutes. Dough will pull away from side of bowl although still stick to bottom. Lift dough out of bowl and slap back into bowl 10 times.

● Scrape dough onto well-floured surface; knead briefly to form soft ball. Place, seam side down, in greased bowl, turning to grease all over. Cover with plastic wrap; let rise in warm draft-free place until doubled in bulk, about 1-1/2 hours.

● Turn out dough onto well-floured surface. Press lightly to deflate some, but not all, air bubbles. Gently shape into 2 rounds by pulling edges of dough over center and pinching to seal.

● Line two 4- to 6-cup (1 to 1.5 L) bowls or baskets with tea towels; dust towels well all over with flour. Place each round, seam side up, in bowl; fold towel over loosely to cover. Let rise until doubled in bulk and bubbles appear at surface, 1 to 1-1/2 hours.

● Using towel, gently turn out dough, seam side down, onto floured baking sheet. With sharp knife, cut four 1/2-inch (1 cm) deep slashes on top of each loaf. Bake in center of 450°F (230°C) oven for 10 minutes. Immediately reduce heat to 400°F (200°C); bake for about 25 minutes longer or until golden brown and loaves sound hollow when tapped on bottom. Turn oven off; let loaves stand in oven for 5 minutes. Let cool on racks. Makes 2 small loaves, 8 slices each.

VARIATIONS

● For 1 large loaf, let rise second time in 8-cup (2 L) bowl or basket. Increase baking time at 400°F (200°C) to 45 minutes.

● You can replace 1 cup (250 mL) of the all-purpose flour with 1-1/4 cups (300 mL) whole wheat flour, if you prefer an even more rustic loaf.

TIP: Instead of kneading dough by slapping, you can knead it in a heavy-duty mixer at low speed for 15 minutes. Knead at high speed for 1 minute. Shape and let rise as directed.

LEFTOVER BREAD

Since many breads and flatbreads are low in fat, they do not keep well, especially in hot humid weather. It's a good idea to cube leftover bread or to slice it thinly and turn it into a resource — croutons or Melba toast.

● Spread in a single layer on ungreased baking sheets and toast in 325°F (160°C) oven until golden and crisp.

● For flavored croutons, cut bread or flatbread into thick slices. Brush lightly with a mixture of olive oil and whatever seasoning you like: sage, basil, rosemary, Italian herb seasoning, chile spices or minced garlic. Cut into cubes and toast as above.

ADAPTING YOUR FAVORITE BREAD RECIPES

Make use of your appliances to enjoy homemade bread more often.

FOR YOUR BREAD MACHINE

It may take a number of attempts to get the formula for your favorite recipe just right for your bread machine. Write down the quantities that work for you.

● Using the manufacturer's manual as a guide, determine the amount of flour (number of cups) that you can use in your bread machine. You must not exceed this amount or you might damage the machine.

● For each 1 cup (250 mL) flour used, you will need approximately 1/3 cup (75 mL) liquid, at least 1 tsp (5 mL) sugar, honey or other sweetener, 1/4 tsp (1 mL) salt and 1/2 tsp (2 mL) bread-machine or quick-rising (instant) dry yeast. Do not leave out the sweetener or the salt: both are needed for successful yeast dough.

● Have all ingredients at room temperature for best results.

● If fat is called for in the recipe, use at least 1 tsp (5 mL) room-temperature solid fat or vegetable oil per 1 cup (250 mL) flour.

● Remove the bread pan from the bread machine before adding any ingredients. Add ingredients to the pan in the order suggested by the machine's manufacturer or according to the recipe you are following. Yeast must remain dry until the machine starts to mix ingredients.

● Be present when the bread machine starts to knead the ingredients. Open the lid and look at the dough ball during the first knead: If it is too firm and dry, or if the bread machine seems to be straining, add a few drops of liquid to make it softer; if it is too sticky, add enough flour to make it smooth. Keep track of what you are adding and change your basic recipe accordingly for the next time.

FOR YOUR FOOD PROCESSOR

● Be careful not to exceed the amount of flour that your food processor can handle. Use either the steel knife or the dough blade according to the amount of flour and the manufacturer's recommendations.

● Measure dry ingredients, including quick-rising (instant) dry yeast if using, into work bowl with correct blade in place. Cut in solid fat using pulse motion.

● With machine running, pour warm liquid ingredients (including softened yeast mixture if using active dry yeast) through feed tube in a slow steady stream until a ball of dough forms. Add flour or liquid as needed to make dough smooth, not sticky or tough.

● Knead dough by continuing to process for 30 to 60 seconds, depending on the recipe. Dough should be smooth and elastic.

● If the steel blade is used, knead in ingredients such as fruit or nuts by hand after dough is removed from food processor to keep them from becoming too finely chopped.

FOR YOUR HEAVY-DUTY MIXER

● Use mixer's dough hook attachment.

● Measure 1/2 to 1 cup (125 to 250 mL) of the flour; set aside. Measure all other dry ingredients, including quick-rising (instant) yeast if using, into mixing bowl. If using active dry yeast, soften in water as indicated in recipe.

● Mix liquid ingredients together. With mixer running at low speed, slowly pour liquid ingredients over dry, adding reserved flour as needed to make a ball of dough.

● Knead dough by running mixer at low speed, adding flour occasionally if necessary, for 8 to 10 minutes or until dough is smooth and elastic.

Country Potato Bread ▲

Rustic touches include a floured top and crisscross design. But looks are not all. The texture, similar to sourdough, makes these loaves perfect partners for hearty soups and summer salads.

Per slice: about
- 104 calories
- 1 g fat
- 3 g protein
- 21 g carbohydrate

2	small potatoes, peeled (8 oz/250 g total)	2
1 tsp	granulated sugar	5 mL
1/4 cup	warm water	50 mL
1	pkg active dry yeast	1
1 tbsp	salt	15 mL
1 tbsp	lard or shortening, melted and cooled	15 mL
3 cups	(approx) all-purpose flour	750 mL
2 cups	whole wheat flour	500 mL
	Cornmeal	

● In saucepan of boiling water, cook potatoes until tender. Drain, reserving 1-1/2 cups (375 mL) cooking liquid. Let cooking liquid cool to lukewarm; mash potatoes and set aside.

● In large bowl, dissolve sugar in warm water. Sprinkle in yeast; let stand for 10 minutes or until frothy. Whisk in mashed potatoes, reserved lukewarm cooking liquid, salt, lard and 1 cup (250 mL) of the all-purpose flour. With wooden spoon, gradually stir in whole wheat flour and enough of the remaining all-purpose flour to make dough that holds together but is still soft.

● Turn out dough onto lightly floured surface; knead in enough of the remaining flour for about 10 minutes or until smooth and elastic. Place in greased bowl, turning to grease all over. Cover with plastic wrap; let rise in warm draft-free place until doubled in bulk, 1-1/2 to 2 hours.

● Punch down dough; turn out onto lightly floured surface. Knead into smooth ball. Divide dough in half; shape each half into round loaf, stretching dough down all around and tucking underneath to shape. Dust tops with flour. Place loaves on baking sheets sprinkled with cornmeal. Cover and let rise until doubled in bulk, 45 to 60 minutes.

● Using serrated knife, make shallow crisscross slashes across top of loaves. Bake in center of 375°F (190°C) oven for 40 to 45 minutes or until golden brown and loaves sound hollow when tapped on bottom. Let cool on racks. Makes 2 loaves, 12 slices each.

Do-the-Mashed-Potato Bread

1	small potato, peeled and halved	1
3 tbsp	vegetable oil	50 mL
2 tbsp	granulated sugar	25 mL
1-1/2 tsp	salt	7 mL
3 cups	all-purpose flour	750 mL
1-1/2 tsp	quick-rising (instant) dry yeast (or 1-1/4 tsp/6 mL bread machine yeast)	7 mL

● In saucepan of boiling salted water, cook potato for 10 to 15 minutes or until tender; drain, reserving 3/4 cup (175 mL) cooking liquid. Mash potato well to make 1/2 cup (125 mL). Let potato and reserved cooking liquid cool to room temperature.

● Into pan of 1-1/2 to 2 lb (750 g to 1 kg) bread machine, add (in order) cooking liquid, oil, sugar, salt, mashed potato, flour and yeast. (Do not let yeast touch liquid.) Choose nonsweet- or nonfresh-milk bread setting. Let baked loaf cool on rack. Makes 1 loaf, 12 slices.

Yeast thrives on starch, not only in flour, but also in mashed potatoes. This traditional ingredient — once used to stretch scarce, more expensive wheat — helps produce an airy, even-textured loaf. Potato bread makes superlative sandwiches and toast.

Per slice: about
- 160 calories
- 4 g protein
- 4 g fat
- 28 g carbohydrate

Buttermilk Loaf

Pinch	granulated sugar	Pinch
1/3 cup	warm water	75 mL
2-1/2 tsp	active dry yeast	12 mL
2 cups	buttermilk	500 mL
1/3 cup	butter, melted	75 mL
2 tbsp	liquid honey	25 mL
1	egg, beaten	1
6 cups	(approx) all-purpose flour	1.5 L
1-1/2 tsp	salt	7 mL
1 tbsp	milk	15 mL

● In large bowl, dissolve sugar in warm water. Sprinkle in yeast; let stand for 10 minutes or until frothy. Stir in buttermilk, butter, honey and egg. With wooden spoon, stir in 3 cups (750 mL) of the flour and salt, beating until smooth. Gradually stir in 2-3/4 cups (675 mL) of the remaining flour to form slightly moist dough.

● Turn out dough onto lightly floured surface; knead for 8 minutes or until smooth and elastic, dusting with as much of the remaining flour as necessary to keep dough from sticking.

● Place dough in greased bowl, turning to grease all over. Cover with plastic wrap; let rise in warm draft-free place until doubled in bulk, 1 to 1-1/2 hours.

● Punch down dough; turn out onto lightly floured surface. Divide in half; knead each into ball. Cover with tea towel; let rest for 5 minutes. Press each into rectangle. Starting at narrow end, roll up into cylinder; pinch along bottom to smooth and seal. Place each in greased 9- x 5-inch (2 L) loaf pan. Cover and let rise for 1 to 1-1/2 hours or until 1/2 inch (1 cm) above rim of pan and dough does not spring back when lightly pressed.

● Brush top of each loaf with milk. With sharp knife, cut slash about 3/4 inch (2 cm) deep along length of top. Bake in 350°F (180°C) oven for 45 to 55 minutes or until golden brown and loaves sound hollow when tapped on bottom. Remove from pans; let cool on racks. Makes 2 loaves, 12 slices each.

This glossy Canadian classic combines a fine, even texture, mild dairy tang and a warm caramel color. Enjoy it as an excellent sandwich bread.

Per slice: about
- 150 calories
- 4 g protein
- 3 g fat
- 27 g carbohydrate

Traditional Challah ▶

The Jewish Sabbath meal is traditionally graced with challah — a braided egg bread. The bread resonates with deeper meaning at the Jewish New Year, when the challah is shaped into a crown. The addition of sweet raisins is an extra guarantee of a special and lucky year.

Per slice: about
- 191 calories
- 5 g protein
- 5 g fat
- 32 g carbohydrate

2 tsp	granulated sugar	10 mL
1/2 cup	warm water	125 mL
1	pkg active dry yeast (or 1 tbsp/15 mL)	1
3-1/2 cups	(approx) all-purpose flour	875 mL
1 tsp	salt	5 mL
1/4 cup	liquid honey	50 mL
2	eggs, lightly beaten	2
2	egg yolks	2
1/4 cup	butter, melted, or vegetable oil	50 mL
3/4 cup	golden raisins	175 mL
	TOPPING	
1	egg yolk, lightly beaten	1
1 tbsp	sesame seeds	15 mL

● In large bowl, dissolve sugar in warm water. Sprinkle in yeast; let stand for 10 minutes or until frothy. With wooden spoon, stir in 3 cups (750 mL) of the flour and salt; stir in honey, eggs, egg yolks and butter until dough forms.

● Turn out dough onto lightly floured surface; knead for 10 minutes or until smooth and elastic, adding enough of the remaining flour as necessary. Place in greased bowl, turning to grease all over. Cover with plastic wrap; let rise in warm draft-free place until doubled in bulk, about 1 hour. Punch down dough; knead in raisins. Let rest for 5 minutes.

● TO MAKE CROWN: Roll dough into 30-inch (76 cm) long rope. Holding one end in place, wind remaining rope around end to form fairly tight spiral that is slightly higher in center. Transfer to lightly greased baking sheet.

● TO MAKE BRAID: Divide dough into quarters; roll each into 18-inch (45 cm) long rope. Place ropes side by side on greased baking sheet; pinch together at one end. Starting at pinched end, move second rope from left over rope on its right. Move far right rope over two ropes on left. Move far left rope over two ropes on right. Repeat until braid is complete; tuck ends under braid.

● Cover crown loaf or braid loaf with plastic wrap. Let rise in warm draft-free place until doubled in bulk, about 1 hour.

● TOPPING: Stir egg yolk with 1 tsp (5 mL) water; brush over loaf. Sprinkle with sesame seeds. Bake in center of 350°F (180°C) oven for 35 to 45 minutes or until golden brown and loaf sounds hollow when tapped on bottom. Let cool on rack. Makes 1 loaf, 16 slices.

BREAD MACHINE METHOD
(for dough only)
● Replace active dry yeast with 2-1/2 tsp (12 mL) quick-rising (instant) dry yeast. Into pan of machine, add (in order) water, honey, sugar, butter, eggs, egg yolks, salt, flour and yeast. (Do not let yeast touch liquid.) Choose dough setting. When complete, remove from pan. Knead in raisins. Let rest for 5 minutes. Shape and bake as directed.

GETTING A RISE
● Recipes use either active dry yeast that is usually softened in a slightly sweet, slightly warm liquid (110°F/45°C) before making dough or quick-rising (instant) dry yeast that is usually blended right into the flour. Liquid added is warmer (120 to 130°F/50 to 55°C), but still comfortable to the touch. Bread machine yeast has added ascorbic acid to improve the yeast performance.
● Buy yeast in packages, cans or jars depending on the frequency of your bread baking. Always store yeast in the refrigerator and respect the best-before date to ensure success.
● Cubes of fresh yeast are available in the refrigerator section of some supermarkets. Use as you would active dry yeast and dissolve in sweetened lukewarm water according to the recipe.

Rustic Cracked Wheat Bread

"Pain de campagne" is how Montreal food editor Julian Armstrong describes these cracked wheat rounds — crusty on the outside and blissfully chewy on the inside.

Per slice: about
- 137 calories
- 4 g protein
- trace fat
- 29 g carbohydrate

1 cup	coarse cracked wheat	250 mL
6 cups	all-purpose flour	1.5 L
1	pkg quick-rising (instant) dry yeast (or 1 tbsp/15 mL)	1
1 tbsp	granulated sugar	15 mL
2 tsp	salt	10 mL
2 cups	warm water	500 mL

● In large bowl, pour 3 cups (750 mL) boiling water over cracked wheat. Let stand for 30 minutes; drain.

● Meanwhile, in another large bowl, combine half of the flour, the yeast, sugar, salt and warm water; beat with electric mixer for about 3 minutes or until smooth and elastic. Cover with plastic wrap; let rise in warm draft-free place for 30 to 40 minutes or until bubbly and light.

● Stir down dough. With wooden spoon, stir in cracked wheat and enough of the remaining flour to make soft dough. Turn out onto lightly floured surface; knead for 8 to 10 minutes or until smooth and elastic. Place in greased bowl, turning to grease all over. Cover with plastic wrap; let rise in warm draft-free place until doubled in bulk, 45 to 60 minutes.

● Punch down dough; turn out onto lightly floured surface. Knead into smooth ball. Divide dough in half; knead each half into round loaf, stretching dough down all around and tucking underneath to shape. Let rest for 2 minutes. Repeat stretching and tucking to tighten shape. Place on large greased baking sheets. Cover and let rise until doubled in bulk, 40 to 45 minutes.

● Using serrated knife, cut shallow slash in top of each loaf. Bake in center of 450°F (230°C) oven for 20 minutes. Reduce temperature to 375°F (190°C); bake for 20 to 30 minutes or until loaves sound hollow when tapped on bottom. Let cool on racks. Makes 2 loaves, 12 slices each.

Sourdough Starter

Here's the starter for all your future sourdough loaves. As time passes, it matures and develops more complex nuances of flavors.

Per 2 cups (500 mL): about
- 661 calories
- 22 g protein
- 5 g fat
- 128 g carbohydrate
- good source of calcium
- excellent source of iron
- high source of fiber

2 cups	all-purpose flour	500 mL
1 cup	warm water	250 mL
1/4 tsp	active dry yeast	1 mL

● In 8-cup (2 L) container, stir together flour, water and yeast, scraping down side. Cover with plastic wrap; let stand at room temperature for at least 8 hours or for up to 24 hours or until tripled in volume. Refrigerate for 3 days.

● Stir in 1/2 cup (125 mL) milk or water and 1/2 cup (125 mL) all-purpose flour. Refrigerate for 3 more days. Makes about 4 cups (1 L).

● KEEPING: After using half of the starter, refresh (or feed) the remaining starter by stirring in 3/4 cup (175 mL) milk or water and 1-1/4 cups (300 mL) all-purpose flour. Refrigerate for at least 2 days or for up to 1 week.

● FEEDING: Your starter must be fed or refreshed once a week whether you make bread or not. If not making bread, dispose of half the starter and refresh with 3/4 cup (175 mL) water and 1-1/4 cups (300 mL) all-purpose flour.

● FREEZING: Starter can be frozen for up to 3 weeks. Let thaw at room temperature for 3 hours before using.

● EXPERIMENTING: Try using this starter in your favorite bread recipe and see how it affects flavor and texture. Use half the starter to replace 1-1/4 cups (300 mL) all-purpose flour and 3/4 cup (175 mL) water plus half the yeast in a bread recipe calling for a total of 5 to 8 cups (1.25 to 2 L) of flour.

Sourdough Bread

TWO-DAY SOURDOUGH		
Half	batch Sourdough Starter (recipe, p. 20)	Half
3/4 cup	warm water	175 mL
3 cups	(approx) all-purpose flour	750 mL
2 tsp	salt	10 mL
2 tsp	vegetable oil	10 mL
1	egg	1

● In large bowl, stir Sourdough Starter with 1/2 cup (125 mL) of the warm water until well combined. With wooden spoon, beat in 1-1/2 cups (375 mL) of the flour until smooth thick paste forms. Cover with plastic wrap; let rise at room temperature for at least 12 hours or for up to 24 hours.

● Stir in remaining warm water. Stir in 1-1/4 cups (300 mL) more flour and salt until shaggy dough forms. Turn out onto lightly floured surface. Knead for 8 minutes or until smooth, elastic and somewhat moist, dusting with as much of the remaining flour as needed to prevent sticking. Place in greased bowl, turning to grease all over. Cover with plastic wrap; let rise in warm draft-free place until nearly tripled in bulk, about 2 hours.

● Turn out dough onto lightly floured surface. Punch down so very few bubbles remain and dough is in flat circle. Fold top third, then bottom third over center of dough, pressing edges to seal. Fold top edge over to bottom edge, pressing to seal. With hands, roll dough lightly into 14-inch (35 cm) long oval, pushing harder at ends to form points that are narrower than center.

● Place, seam side down, on greased baking sheet; brush with oil. Cover lightly with plastic wrap; let rise in warm draft-free place until doubled in bulk, 1-1/2 to 2 hours.

● Whisk egg with 1 tbsp (15 mL) water; brush over loaf. With sharp knife, slash top diagonally 5 times. Bake in center of 425°F (220°C) oven for about 50 minutes or until golden brown and loaf sounds hollow when tapped on bottom. Makes 1 loaf, 20 slices.

SHORTCUT SOURDOUGH		
Pinch	granulated sugar	Pinch
3/4 cup	warm water	175 mL
1/2 tsp	active dry yeast	2 mL
Half	batch Sourdough Starter (recipe, p. 20)	Half
2-3/4 cups	(approx) all-purpose flour	675 mL
2 tsp	salt	10 mL
2 tsp	vegetable oil	10 mL
1	egg	1

● In large bowl, dissolve sugar in warm water. Sprinkle in yeast; let stand for 10 minutes or until frothy. Stir in Sourdough Starter until well combined. With wooden spoon, stir in flour and salt until shaggy dough forms. Turn out onto lightly floured surface. Knead for 8 minutes or until smooth and elastic, sprinkling with up to 2 tbsp (25 mL) more flour as needed to prevent sticking.

● Place in greased bowl, turning to grease all over. Cover with plastic wrap; let rise in warm draft-free place until doubled in bulk, about 2 hours.

● Shape, let rise and bake as directed. Makes 1 loaf, 20 slices.

Sourdough is the original bread, dating back to the days when a natural yeast starter was used and replenished for years, even generations, to make chewy crusty loaves with a natural tangy aroma and moist, slightly elastic crumb. Be sure to leave yourself plenty of time when making sourdough bread, especially at the beginning before you're into the rhythm of this ancient bread-making technique.

TWO-DAY SOURDOUGH
Per slice: about
- 109 calories
- 1 g fat
- 3 g protein
- 21 g carbohydrate

SHORTCUT SOURDOUGH
Per slice: about
- 86 calories
- 1 g fat
- 3 g protein
- 16 g carbohydrate

Country Seed Bread ▼

Sesame, flax and poppy seeds update and enhance a loaf that uses both whole wheat and all-purpose flours.

Per slice: about
- 172 calories
- 6 g protein
- 5 g fat
- 28 g carbohydrate

TIP: For a nuttier flavor, toast seeds on baking sheet in 350°F (180°C) oven for 4 minutes; let cool completely.

2 cups	(approx) all-purpose flour	500 mL
1 cup	whole wheat flour	250 mL
1/4 cup	flax seeds	50 mL
2 tbsp	sesame seeds	25 mL
1 tbsp	poppy seeds	15 mL
2 tsp	quick-rising (instant) dry yeast	10 mL
1-1/4 cups	warm water	300 mL
2 tbsp	liquid honey	25 mL
2 tbsp	vegetable oil	25 mL
1-1/2 tsp	salt	7 mL

● In large bowl, stir together all-purpose and whole wheat flours, flax, sesame and poppy seeds and yeast. In small bowl, whisk together water, honey, oil and salt; stir into flour mixture until sticky dough forms.

● Turn out dough onto lightly floured surface. Knead for about 8 minutes or until still slightly sticky and dough springs back when pressed in center, adding up to 1/4 cup (50 mL) more all-purpose flour as necessary. Place in greased bowl, turning to grease all over. Cover with plastic wrap; let rise in warm draft-free place until doubled in bulk, about 1-1/4 hours.

● Punch down dough; turn out onto lightly floured surface. Gently pull dough into 11- x 8-inch (28 x 20 cm) rectangle. Starting at one narrow end, roll up into cylinder; pinch along bottom to smooth and seal. Fit into greased 8- x 4-inch (1.5 L) loaf pan. Cover and let rise until doubled in bulk and about 3/4 inch (2 cm) above rim of pan, about 1 hour.

● Brush top of loaf with water. With serrated knife, make one 1-inch (2.5 cm) deep cut lengthwise along top of loaf. Bake in center of 400°F (200°C) oven for 15 minutes. Reduce heat to 350°F (180°C); bake for 30 to 35 minutes or until browned and loaf sounds hollow when tapped on bottom. Remove from pan; let cool on rack. Makes 1 loaf, 12 slices.

LARGE BREAD MACHINE METHOD 🗔

● Into pan of 1-1/2 to 2 lb (750 g to 1 kg) machine, add (in order) water, honey, oil, salt, all-purpose and whole wheat flours, flax seeds, sesame seeds, poppy seeds and yeast. (Do not let yeast touch liquid.) Choose appropriate setting (whole wheat, powdered milk). Let baked loaf cool on rack. Makes 1 loaf.

SMALL BREAD MACHINE METHOD 🗔

● Into pan of 1 lb (500 g) machine, add (in order) 3/4 cup (175 mL) warm water, 4 tsp (20 mL) each liquid honey and vegetable oil, 1 tsp (5 mL) salt, 1-1/3 cups (325 mL) all-purpose flour, 2/3 cup (150 mL) whole wheat flour, 3 tbsp (50 mL) flax seeds, 4 tsp (20 mL) sesame seeds, 2 tsp (10 mL) poppy seeds and 1-1/4 tsp (6 mL) quick-rising (instant) dry yeast. (Do not let yeast touch liquid.) Choose appropriate setting (whole wheat, powdered milk). Let baked loaf cool on rack. Makes 1 small loaf, 8 slices.

Wild Rice Many-Grain Bread

1/2 cup	wild rice	125 mL
2 tbsp	granulated sugar	25 mL
1/4 cup	warm water	50 mL
1	pkg active dry yeast (or 1 tbsp/15 mL)	1
5 cups	(approx) all-purpose flour	1.25 L
1/4 cup	fancy molasses	50 mL
2 tbsp	shortening	25 mL
1 tsp	salt	5 mL
1/2 cup	natural bran	125 mL
1/2 cup	raw sunflower seeds	125 mL
3/4 cup	7-grain cereal	175 mL
3/4 cup	rolled oats	175 mL

● In saucepan, cook wild rice in 2 cups (500 mL) water for about 45 minutes or until tender; drain and let cool.

● Meanwhile, dissolve 1 tsp (5 mL) of the sugar in warm water. Sprinkle in yeast; let soften, stirring together until dissolved. Stir in 1/4 cup (50 mL) of the flour to make thin paste; set in warm place for 10 minutes or until bubbly.

● In large bowl and using electric mixer, combine molasses, remaining sugar, shortening, salt and 2 cups (500 mL) warm water. In order, beat in bran, sunflower seeds, yeast mixture, wild rice, 7-grain cereal and rolled oats. With wooden spoon, beat in as much of the remaining flour as necessary to make firm dough. Turn out onto lightly floured surface; knead for about 10 minutes or until smooth and elastic, kneading in as much of the remaining flour as necessary.

● Place in large greased bowl, turning to grease all over. Cover with plastic wrap; let rise in warm draft-free place until doubled in bulk, about 2 hours.

● Punch down dough; turn out onto lightly floured surface. Divide into thirds. With rolling pin, flatten each to about 7-1/2-inch (19 cm) square; firmly roll up each into log. Place each in greased 8- x 4-inch (1.5 L) loaf pan. Cover and let rise until doubled in bulk, about 1-1/2 hours.

● Bake in center of 375°F (190°C) oven for 25 minutes or until loaves sound hollow when tapped on bottom. Remove from pans; let cool on racks. Makes 3 loaves, 12 slices each.

F*rom chef Bertha Skye comes a nutty-flavored loaf starring wild rice, a delicious ingredient grown in northern Saskatchewan.*

Per slice: about
- 117 calories
- 4 g protein
- 2 g fat
- 21 g carbohydrate

BREAD-MACHINE BASICS

1 Read your manual. Every bread machine is different. Be sure you are using the correct setting or cycle on your machine.

2 Add the ingredients to the pan in the order recommended in the manual for your machine.

3 Place machine well away from counter edge. Occasionally, a machine will move during the knead cycle.

4 Do not open lid of machine once the proof cycle begins. If you must peek, do so while the machine is kneading dough.

5 If a baked loaf sticks to the pan, rap a top corner of the pan against the countertop to help shake bread loose, or use a plastic spatula to ease out loaf. Don't use a knife or metal spatula; you may damage the nonstick coating.

6 If the blade is stuck in the loaf, use a small knife to pry it loose.

7 If the blade sticks to the pan, soak in warm water for 15 minutes, then remove.

8 If the crust is too dark, use the setting for sweet bread on your machine.

9 Store bread at room temperature in an airtight plastic bag, or freeze.

Caraway Rye Bread

Caraway seeds spike a mild rye-flavored loaf that bakes up into a shiny dome. The secret of its dusky color? Molasses and dark rye flour, of course, plus a measure of rich brown cocoa.

Per slice: about
- 150 calories
- 5 g protein
- 3 g fat
- 27 g carbohydrate

TIP: Crush caraway seeds on cutting board by firmly pressing with bottom of heavy saucepan.

1 tsp	packed brown sugar	5 mL
1 cup	warm water	250 mL
4 tsp	active dry yeast	20 mL
1 cup	warm milk	250 mL
1/4 cup	fancy molasses	50 mL
1/4 cup	butter, softened	50 mL
1 tbsp	cider vinegar	15 mL
1/2 tsp	salt	2 mL
2 tbsp	unsweetened cocoa powder	25 mL
2 tbsp	caraway seeds, crushed	25 mL
4 cups	(approx) all-purpose flour	1 L
2 cups	rye flour	500 mL
1	egg, lightly beaten	1

● In large bowl, dissolve brown sugar in warm water. Sprinkle in yeast; let stand for 10 minutes or until frothy. Whisk in milk, molasses, butter, vinegar and salt. With electric mixer, beat in cocoa, caraway seeds, 2-1/2 cups (625 mL) of the all-purpose flour and rye flour until smooth. With wooden spoon, gradually stir in 1 cup (250 mL) of the remaining flour to make soft but not sticky dough.

● Turn out dough onto lightly floured surface; knead for 8 to 10 minutes or until smooth and elastic, adding more flour as necessary. Place in greased bowl, turning to grease all over. Cover with plastic wrap; let rise in warm draft-free place until doubled in bulk, about 1 hour.

● Punch down dough; turn out onto lightly floured surface. Knead into ball. Divide dough in half; shape each into ball. Gently pull each ball into 11- x 8-inch (28 x 20 cm) rectangle. Starting at narrow end, roll up into cylinder; pinch along bottom to smooth and seal. Fit into two greased 8- x 4-inch (1.5 L) loaf pans. Brush with egg. Cover and let rise in warm draft-free place until doubled in bulk, about 1 hour.

● Bake in center of 350°F (180°C) oven for 35 to 45 minutes or until golden brown and loaves sound hollow when tapped on bottom. Remove from pans; let cool on racks. Makes 2 loaves, 12 slices each.

Ballymaloe Whole Wheat Bread

When Vancouver food writer Ruth Phelan studied at Ireland's famous cooking school, Ballymaloe, she learned how to make this moist, nutty-flavored, no-knead, one-rise bread. Enjoy it toasted with butter and berry jam.

Per slice: about
- 126 calories
- 5 g protein
- 1 g fat
- 26 g carbohydrate
- high source of fiber

2 cups	(approx) warm water	500 mL
3 tbsp	fancy molasses	50 mL
1	pkg active dry yeast (or 1 tbsp/15 mL)	1
3-1/2 cups	whole wheat flour	875 mL
1/4 cup	wheat germ	50 mL
2 tsp	salt	10 mL
1 tbsp	sesame seeds	15 mL

● Cut 13- x 8-inch (32 x 20 cm) piece of parchment paper; make 3-inch (8 cm) slash into each corner. Fit into greased 9- x 5-inch (2 L) loaf pan and trim excess paper. Set aside.

● In large bowl, stir 1 cup (250 mL) of the warm water with molasses. Sprinkle in yeast; let stand for 10 minutes or until frothy. With wooden spoon, beat in flour, wheat germ, salt and enough of the remaining water to make sticky dough. Work with hands for 30 seconds.

● Transfer to prepared pan. Sprinkle with sesame seeds. Cover with plastic wrap; let rise in warm draft-free place just until dough reaches top of pan, about 20 minutes.

● Bake in center of 400°F (200°C) oven for 50 to 60 minutes or until browned and loaf sounds hollow when tapped on bottom. Remove from pan; peel off paper. Turn upside down and return to turned-off oven for 20 minutes. Let cool on rack. Makes 1 loaf, 14 slices.

Crusty Bran Bread ▲

1-1/4 cups	water	300 mL
2 tbsp	packed brown sugar	25 mL
2 tbsp	fancy molasses	25 mL
2 tbsp	butter, melted	25 mL
1-1/2 tsp	salt	7 mL
3-1/4 cups	all-purpose flour	800 mL
1 cup	natural bran	250 mL
1-1/2 tsp	quick-rising (instant) dry yeast (or 1-1/4 tsp/6 mL bread machine yeast)	7 mL

● Into pan of 2 lb (1 kg) bread machine, add (in order) water, brown sugar, molasses, butter, salt, flour, bran and yeast. (Do not let yeast touch liquid.) Choose basic or white bread setting. Let baked loaf cool on rack. Makes 1 loaf, 12 slices.

SMALL BREAD MACHINE METHOD
● Into pan of 1 to 1-1/2 lb (500 to 750 g) bread machine, add (in order) 3/4 cup (175 mL) water, 1 tbsp (15 mL) each brown sugar, molasses and melted butter, 1 tsp (5 mL) salt, 2 cups (500 mL) all-purpose flour, 2/3 cup (150 mL) bran and 1 tsp (5 mL) quick-rising (instant) dry yeast (or 3/4 tsp/4 mL bread machine yeast). (Do not let yeast touch liquid.) Choose basic or white bread setting. Let baked loaf cool on rack. Makes 1 small loaf, 8 slices.

Per slice: about • 155 calories • 4 g protein • 2 g fat • 31 g carbohydrate

I*t's easy to get into the habit of fresh good-for-your-health bread when you have a bread machine. Small households, daunted by big bakery loaves, especially like the convenience of a small, warm and crusty loaf every day or two. What a great waker-upper!*

Per slice: about
• 170 calories   • 5 g protein
• 3 g fat   • 34 g carbohydrate

Celebration Breads

Bread rises to every special occasion — so get ready to celebrate with sweet loaves bursting with fruit and nuts, or savory breads rich with the flavors of herbs, caramelized onion, cheese, smoky meats and more.

Panettone ▶

H*igh-domed golden panettone is the traditional Christmas dessert bread all over Italy and in every Italo-Canadian community. Lavish with golden raisins, citrus peel, eggs and butter, it epitomizes the richness and generosity of the season.*

Per slice: about
• 195 calories   • 4 g protein
• 7 g fat   • 27 g carbohydrate

TIP: Baking panettone in a variety of can sizes is not traditional but does allow you to share some of this splendid treat with those at the top of your gift list. For small panettone, use 10 to 28 oz (284 to 796 mL) cans. Make ball of dough small enough to fill can just under halfway. Let rise as in recipe; bake for 30 to 40 minutes.

3/4 cup	golden raisins	175 mL
1/2 cup	candied mixed peel	125 mL
1/2 cup	candied citron	125 mL
8-3/4 cups	(approx) all-purpose flour	2.175 L
1 cup	granulated sugar	250 mL
3/4 cup	warm milk	175 mL
2	pkg active dry yeast (or 2 tbsp/25 mL)	2
6	eggs	6
6	egg yolks	6
1 tbsp	each grated orange and lemon rind	15 mL
1 tbsp	vanilla	15 mL
1-1/2 tsp	salt	7 mL
1-1/2 cups	unsalted butter, softened	375 mL

● In small bowl, combine raisins, candied peel and citron. Add 2 tbsp (25 mL) of the flour; toss to coat. Set aside. In separate bowl, dissolve 1 tsp (5 mL) of the sugar in warm milk. Sprinkle in yeast; let stand for 10 minutes or until frothy.

● Whisk together eggs, egg yolks, orange and lemon rinds and vanilla until combined; stir into milk mixture. In large bowl, stir together 4 cups (1 L) of the flour, remaining sugar and salt. With wooden spoon, stir in egg mixture all at once. Add butter all at once; stir until blended. Gradually stir in remaining flour to make soft somewhat lumpy dough.

● Turn out dough onto lightly floured surface; knead for about 8 minutes or until soft, smooth and elastic, adding up to 1/3 cup (75 mL) more flour if needed. Lightly dust with flour; cover with tea towel and let rest for 5 minutes.

● Flatten dough into 15-inch (38 cm) circle; top with raisin mixture. Fold dough over mixture; pinch to seal. Knead for 2 to 3 minutes or until raisin mixture is evenly distributed. Place in large greased bowl, turning to grease all over. Cover with plastic wrap; let rise in warm draft-free place until doubled in bulk, 1-1/2 to 2 hours.

● Grease two 2 lb (1 kg) coffee cans or panettone moulds. If using cans, line bottoms and sides with parchment paper to extend 1 inch (2.5 cm) above top; wrap outsides and bottoms with double thickness of foil.

● Punch down dough; turn out onto lightly floured surface. Divide in half; roll each into ball. Place, seam side down, in can. Cover and let rise in warm draft-free place until doubled in bulk, about 1-1/2 hours.

● With serrated knife, cut X on top of each loaf. Bake on baking sheet on lowest rack of 350°F (180°C) oven for about 1 hour or until knife inserted in center comes out clean, covering tops lightly with foil if browning too quickly. Let cool in cans on rack for 1 hour. Remove from cans by gently pulling paper; let cool completely on rack. Makes 2 loaves, 24 slices each.

Christmas Stollen ◀

1/2 cup	granulated sugar	125 mL
1-1/4 cups	warm milk	300 mL
2	pkg active dry yeast (or 2 tbsp/25 mL)	2
2	eggs, beaten	2
5 cups	(approx) all-purpose flour	1.25 mL
1-1/2 tsp	salt	7 mL
Pinch	each cinnamon, nutmeg and cardamom	Pinch
3/4 cup	unsalted butter, softened	175 mL
1 cup	raisins	250 mL
1/2 cup	mixed candied peel	125 mL
1/2 cup	candied cherries, chopped	125 mL
1/2 cup	toasted slivered almonds	125 mL
1 tsp	grated lemon rind	5 mL
1	egg white, lightly beaten	1
1/4 cup	butter, melted	50 mL
1/3 cup	icing sugar	75 mL

● In small bowl, dissolve 1 tsp (5 mL) of the sugar in warm milk. Sprinkle in yeast; let stand for 10 minutes or until frothy. Stir in eggs.

● In large bowl, stir together 3 cups (750 mL) of the flour, remaining sugar, salt, cinnamon, nutmeg and cardamom; stir in milk mixture. Drop in softened butter all at once, stirring with wooden spoon until blended. Stir in remaining flour to make soft somewhat lumpy dough.

● Turn out dough onto lightly floured surface; knead for 10 to 12 minutes or until smooth and elastic, adding up to 3 tbsp (50 mL) more flour if needed. Lightly dust with flour; cover with tea towel and let rest for 5 minutes. Meanwhile, in small bowl, stir together raisins, candied peel, candied cherries, almonds and lemon rind.

● Flatten dough into rectangle; sprinkle two-thirds with one-half of the raisin mixture. Fold dough over in thirds; knead until raisin mixture is evenly distributed, about 4 minutes. Cover and let rest for 5 minutes. Repeat with remaining raisin mixture. Place dough in greased bowl, turning to grease all over; cover with plastic wrap and let rise in warm draft-free place until doubled in bulk, about 1-1/2 hours.

● Punch down dough; turn out onto lightly floured surface. Divide in half; shape each half into 8-inch (20 cm) long log. With long side closest, roll out to 1/2-inch (1 cm) thickness, leaving 1-inch (2.5 cm) border unrolled at top and bottom.

● Brush egg white over each; fold bottom half of dough up to top, aligning raised borders side by side. Place on two lightly greased baking sheets. Cover and let rise in warm draft-free place until doubled in bulk, about 1 hour.

● Bake in center of 350°F (180°C) oven for about 45 minutes or until loaves sound hollow when tapped on bottom. Transfer to racks; brush all over with melted butter. Let cool. Dust with icing sugar. *(Loaves can be stored in plastic bags at room temperature for up to 3 days or wrapped in plastic wrap and frozen in rigid airtight container for up to 1 month.)* Makes 2 loaves, 12 slices each.

Christmas in a German deli means beautifully wrapped, icing sugar-dusted and sweetly spiced loaves, each with a characteristic crease along the side. Like British Christmas cake, the abundance of fruit in stollen helps keep the loaf moist for many seasonal servings.

Per slice: about
- 262 calories
- 5 g protein
- 10 g fat
- 39 g carbohydrate

Cranberry Eggnog Bread ▼

Put this tall, cylindrical loaf on your list of gifts from the kitchen. It's impressive to look at — try wrapping it with a wide ribbon — and even more delicious to slice and eat. Makes great French toast, too!

Per slice: about
- 64 calories
- 3 g fat
- 4 g protein
- 30 g carbohydrate

Pinch	granulated sugar	Pinch
1 cup	warm water	250 mL
1	pkg quick-rising (instant) dry yeast (or 1 tbsp/15 mL)	1
5-1/2 cups	(approx) all-purpose flour	1.375 L
2	eggs	2
3	egg yolks	3
1/3 cup	liquid honey	75 mL
3 tbsp	vegetable oil	50 mL
2 tbsp	dark rum (optional)	25 mL
2 tsp	nutmeg	10 mL
1-1/2 tsp	salt	7 mL
1 cup	dried cranberries or golden raisins	250 mL
1	egg white	1

● In large bowl, dissolve sugar in warm water. Sprinkle in yeast; let stand for 10 minutes or until frothy. Whisk in 2-1/2 cups (625 mL) of the flour until smooth. With electric mixer, beat in eggs, egg yolks, honey, oil, rum (if using), nutmeg and salt. With wooden spoon, stir in 2-1/4 cups (550 mL) more flour to make soft slightly sticky dough.

● Turn out dough onto lightly floured surface. Knead for 6 to 8 minutes or until smooth and elastic, adding up to 3/4 cup (175 mL) more flour if needed. Cover with tea towel; let rest for 5 minutes.

● Press out into 12- x 8-inch (30 x 20 cm) rectangle; sprinkle with cranberries. Roll up and knead for 2 to 3 minutes or until cranberries are evenly distributed. Place in greased bowl, turning to grease all over. Cover with plastic wrap; let rise in warm draft-free place until almost doubled in bulk, about 1-1/4 hours.

● Grease two 1.5 L juice cans; line bottoms and sides with parchment paper to extend 1/2 inch (1 cm) above top.

● Punch down dough; turn out onto lightly floured surface. Knead into ball; divide in half. Shape each into ball; gently roll into 4-inch (10 cm) diameter cylinder. Place in cans. Cover and let rise in warm draft-free place until about two-thirds up side of can, about 40 minutes.

● Brush tops with egg white. Bake in center of 375°F (190°C) oven for 40 minutes or until golden brown and loaves sound hollow when tapped on bottom. Remove from cans; let cool on racks. Makes 2 loaves, 12 slices each.

BREAD MACHINE METHOD

● If you wish to omit the rum, increase water to 3/4 cup (175 mL). Into pan of 1-1/2 to 2 lb (750 g to 1 kg) machine, add (in order) 3 egg yolks, 1 egg, 2/3 cup (150 mL) water, 1/4 cup (50 mL) honey, 2 tbsp (25 mL) oil, 4 tsp (20 mL) rum, 1-1/2 tsp (7 mL) salt, 3-1/4 cups (800 mL) flour, 1 tsp (5 mL) nutmeg and 1-1/2 tsp (7 mL) quick-rising (instant) dry yeast. (Do not let yeast touch liquid.) Choose sweet-dough setting, adding 2/3 cup (150 mL) cranberries between first and second kneading. Let baked loaf cool on rack. Makes 1 loaf.

Portuguese Sweet Bread

2 cups	finely chopped mixed candied fruit	500 mL
1 cup	seedless (Lexia) raisins	250 mL
1/2 cup	port	125 mL
2 tsp	each finely grated lemon and orange rind	10 mL
2	pkg active dry yeast (or 2 tbsp/25 mL)	2
3/4 cup	granulated sugar	175 mL
3/4 cup	warm water	175 mL
7 cups	(approx) all-purpose flour	1.75 L
3/4 cup	butter, softened	175 mL
1 tsp	salt	5 mL
4	eggs	4
2/3 cup	warm milk	150 mL
1 cup	toasted chopped almonds or walnuts	250 mL
2 tbsp	butter, melted	25 mL
	TOPPING	
1	egg, lightly beaten	1
2/3 cup	candied cherries, halved	150 mL
3 tbsp	corn syrup	50 mL

● In small bowl, mix together candied fruit, raisins, port and lemon and orange rinds; cover and set aside, stirring occasionally.

● In bowl, whisk together yeast, 1 tbsp (15 mL) of the sugar, warm water and 1 cup (250 mL) of the flour until smooth. Cover with plastic wrap; let rise in warm draft-free place until doubled in bulk, about 30 minutes.

● In large bowl, beat together butter, salt and remaining sugar until fluffy. Beat in eggs, one at a time, beating well after each addition. Beat in 1 cup (250 mL) of the flour; beat in milk. Stir down yeast mixture; beat into egg mixture until blended. With wooden spoon, stir in fruit mixture and nuts. Stir in as much of the remaining flour, 1 cup (250 mL) at a time, as needed to make soft sticky dough.

● Turn out dough onto lightly floured surface. Knead gently for 2 minutes or until smooth and elastic, adding up to 1/2 cup (125 mL) more flour if needed. Place in greased bowl; brush top with butter. Cover with plastic wrap; let rise in warm draft-free place until doubled in bulk, about 1 hour.

● Punch down dough; turn out onto lightly floured surface. Divide in half; knead each half for 1 minute. Shape each into ball; place on greased baking sheet. With two fingers, poke hole in center of each; gently stretch hole to 3-1/2 inches (9 cm) to make about 9-inch (23 cm) ring. Grease outside of two empty 19-oz (540 mL) cans; place can in center of each ring.

● TOPPING: Brush dough with egg. Decoratively arrange cherries over top, pressing into dough. Cover and let rise in warm draft-free place until doubled in bulk, about 1 hour.

● Bake in center of 375°F (190°C) oven for 35 to 40 minutes or until golden. Remove from pan; let cool on rack. *(Loaves can be wrapped in plastic wrap and frozen in rigid airtight container for up to 2 weeks; thaw and reheat in 350°F/180°C oven for 10 minutes.)* Brush corn syrup over loaves. Makes 2 loaves, 20 slices each.

G*lacé fruits such as cherries, pineapple slices or figs can grace the top of this glossy festive bread, shaped either as a spectacular ring or as a braided loaf.*

Per slice: about
- 220 calories
- 4 g protein
- 7 g fat
- 36 g carbohydrate

Orange Poppy Seed Bread Machine Loaf

Instead of setting your alarm, set the bread-machine timer so you can get up in the morning to the homey fragrance of baking bread.

Per slice: about
- 155 calories
- 3 g fat
- 4 g protein
- 28 g carbohydrate

1-1/4 cups	water	300 mL
2 tsp	grated orange rind	10 mL
2 tbsp	packed brown sugar	25 mL
2 tbsp	butter, cubed	25 mL
1 tsp	salt	5 mL
3-1/4 cups	all-purpose flour	800 mL
1 tbsp	poppy seeds	15 mL
1/2 tsp	ground cardamom or nutmeg (optional)	2 mL
3/4 tsp	quick-rising (instant) dry yeast	4 mL

● Into pan of 1-1/2 to 2 lb (750 g to 1 kg) bread machine, add (in order) water, orange rind, sugar, butter, salt, flour, poppy seeds, cardamom (if using) and yeast. (Do not let yeast touch liquid.) Choose basic or regular/light setting. Let baked loaf cool on rack. Makes 1 loaf, 12 slices.

HAND METHOD

● In saucepan, heat together water, orange rind, sugar and butter just until butter starts to melt; set aside. In large bowl, stir together salt, 2 cups (500 mL) of the flour, poppy seeds, cardamom (if using) and 1-1/4 tsp (6 mL) quick-rising (instant) dry yeast. With wooden spoon, stir in butter mixture until smooth. Stir in 1 cup (250 mL) more flour to make soft smooth dough.

● Turn out dough onto lightly floured surface. Knead for about 5 minutes or until smooth and elastic, adding up to 1/4 cup (50 mL) more flour if necessary. Place in greased bowl, turning to grease all over. Cover with plastic wrap; let rise in warm draft-free place until doubled in bulk, about 1 hour.

● Punch down dough; turn out onto lightly floured surface. Press into oval shape. Starting at narrow end, roll up into cylinder; pinch along bottom to smooth and seal. Place, seam side down, in greased 8- x 4-inch (1.5 L) loaf pan. Cover and let rise in warm draft-free place until doubled in bulk, about 1 hour.

● Bake in center of 375°F (190°C) oven for 30 minutes or until golden brown and loaf sounds hollow when tapped on bottom. Remove from pan; let cool on rack. Makes 1 loaf.

FITTING BREAD MAKING INTO YOUR SCHEDULE

1 Start on a day when you are going to be at home attending to other chores. Once the bread is kneaded and sitting in the bowl, pretty well all the work is done. You can carry on with other things between the rising and baking stages.

2 Use your sleeping time! Prepare dough in the evening and let it rise overnight in the refrigerator. After your good night's sleep and your dough's slow flavor-developing rise, the dough is ready to shape and get its second rise, which is usually shorter than the first. However, if you don't want the bread till later that day and you're going to be busy or out, just put the pans in the refrigerator again and the cool temperature will moderate the second rise so the bread is ready to bake when you're ready to enjoy it.

3 In a similar way, you can knead, let rise and shape bread or buns, then stall the baking time by an overnight rest in the fridge. That way, fresh bread or buns can be ready just as sleepyheads make their way to the kitchen. This is an especially good trick for brunch breads.

4 If you're really stuck, enclose the dough in a freezer bag, allowing room for expansion, and freeze the dough until it's convenient to carry on. Let dough thaw and rise in the refrigerator, then shape and bake as directed. (*See Freezing Dough and Bread, p. 33.*)

5 Make use of your bread machine to have bread when you want it — warm and crusty in the morning, or piping hot when you get home from work. Just set the timer.

Double Chocolate Almond Bread

1/2 cup	granulated sugar	125 mL
1/2 cup	warm water	125 mL
1	pkg quick-rising (instant) dry yeast (or 1 tbsp/15 mL)	1
2	eggs	2
1-1/2 cups	milk	375 mL
6-1/4 cups	(approx) all-purpose flour	1.55 L
1/2 cup	sifted unsweetened cocoa powder	125 mL
2 tsp	salt	10 mL
1/4 cup	butter, softened	50 mL
1 cup	chocolate chips	250 mL
1/2 cup	toasted slivered almonds	125 mL

- In large bowl, dissolve a pinch of the sugar in warm water. Sprinkle in yeast; let stand for 10 minutes or until frothy. Whisk in remaining sugar, eggs and milk. Combine 3-1/2 cups (875 mL) of the flour, cocoa and salt; with wooden spoon, stir into egg mixture. Stir in butter until blended. Stir in 2-1/2 cups (625 mL) of the remaining flour, in two additions, to make soft slightly sticky dough.

- Turn out dough onto lightly floured surface; knead for 5 minutes or until smooth and elastic, adding up to 1/4 cup (50 mL) more flour if necessary. Cover with tea towel; let rest for 5 minutes. Press out into 12-inch (30 cm) square; sprinkle with chocolate chips. Roll up and knead for 2 to 3 minutes or until chips are evenly distributed; let rest for 5 minutes. Repeat with slivered almonds. Place in greased bowl, turning to grease all over. Cover with plastic wrap; let rise in warm draft-free place until doubled in bulk, 1-1/2 to 2 hours.

- Punch down dough; turn out onto lightly floured surface. Knead into ball; divide in half. Press each into oval shape. Starting at narrow end, roll up each into cylinder; pinch along bottom to smooth and seal. Place, seam side down, in two greased 8- x 4-inch (1.5 L) loaf pans. Cover and let rise in warm draft-free place until doubled in bulk, 1-1/4 hours.

- Bake in center of 375°F (190°C) oven for 40 to 45 minutes or until loaves sound hollow when tapped on bottom. Let cool in pans on racks for 5 minutes. Remove from pans; let cool on rack. Makes 2 loaves, 12 slices each.

This dark and sophisticated loaf makes any brunch special — or offer it as a truly grown-up dinner-party dessert with whipped mascarpone, fruit and espresso. Dressed up or on its own, it's sure to please old and young alike.

Per slice: about
- 223 calories
- 6 g protein
- 7 g fat
- 35 g carbohydrate

Christmas Kringle ▶

D*anish julekringle, a spectacularly large marzipan-filled, almond-covered pretzel, is served at afternoon or evening coffee parties. The recipe originates with cooking-school teacher Birthe Marie Macdonald who keeps the Christmas traditions of her Danish homeland alive in her Brampton, Ontario, kitchen.*

Per serving: about
- 380 calories
- 7 g protein
- 17 g fat
- 50 g carbohydrate
- good source of iron

1 tsp	granulated sugar	5 mL
1/2 cup	warm water	125 mL
4 tsp	active dry yeast	20 mL
2	eggs	2
1/2 cup	milk	125 mL
1/4 cup	butter, melted	50 mL
2 tbsp	granulated sugar	25 mL
4-1/2 cups	(approx) all-purpose flour	1.125 L
1/4 cup	butter, softened	50 mL
	FILLING	
1/2 cup	butter, softened	125 mL
1/2 cup	icing sugar	125 mL
1/2 cup	amaretto cookie crumbs or dry bread crumbs	125 mL
1/3 cup	chopped almonds	75 mL
1/4 cup	Marzipan (recipe follows)	50 mL
1/2 tsp	almond extract	2 mL
1/2 cup	mixed candied fruit	125 mL
1/2 cup	raisins	125 mL
1	egg, beaten	1
1/3 cup	sliced almonds	75 mL
1/4 cup	granulated sugar	50 mL

● In small bowl, dissolve 1 tsp (5 mL) sugar in warm water. Sprinkle in yeast; let stand for 10 minutes or until frothy. In large bowl, beat together eggs, milk, melted butter and 2 tbsp (25 mL) sugar; beat in yeast mixture. With wooden spoon, beat in 4 cups (1 L) of the flour, 1 cup (250 mL) at a time. Cover with plastic wrap; let rise in warm draft-free place until doubled in bulk, about 1 hour.

● Punch down dough; turn out onto well-floured surface. Using remaining flour as necessary to keep surface well-floured, roll out dough to 16- x 12-inch (40 x 30 cm) rectangle; spread softened butter over half, leaving 1-inch (2.5 cm) border uncovered. Fold uncovered half over dough; pinch edges to seal. With fold to right, roll out to same size rectangle. From short side, fold dough into thirds to make 3 layers; pinch edges to seal.

● FILLING: In bowl, beat butter with icing sugar until creamy; beat in cookie crumbs, almonds, marzipan and almond extract. Roll out dough to 22- x 15-inch (55 x 38 cm) rectangle; cut lengthwise into 3 strips. Spoon one-third of the cookie crumb mixture lengthwise over one outside third of each strip, leaving 1-inch (2.5 cm) border. Sprinkle each with one-third of the candied fruit and raisins. Brush border with some of the egg; fold dough over filling and press to seal.

● Place on large parchment paper-lined or greased baking sheet; shape into pretzel or 3 rings. Brush with remaining egg; sprinkle with almonds and sugar. Cover and let rise in warm draft-free place until doubled in bulk, about 1 hour.

● Bake in center of 375°F (190°C) oven for 20 to 30 minutes or until golden brown. Remove from pan; let cool on rack. *(Kringle can be wrapped in plastic wrap and frozen in rigid airtight container for up to 2 months; thaw and reheat in 350°F/180°C oven for about 10 minutes.)* Makes 16 servings.

MARZIPAN

● In bowl, cover 2 cups (500 mL) unblanched almonds (12 oz/375 g) with boiling water; let stand for 2 minutes. Drain and skin by firmly pressing one end to pop nut through skin. In food processor, grind warm almonds for 1-1/2 to 2 minutes or until fine. Add 2 cups (500 mL) icing sugar; mix for 1 minute or until blended, scraping down side of bowl when necessary. Blend in 2 tsp (10 mL) each almond extract and corn syrup.

● With motor running, pour in enough of 1 lightly beaten egg white to form ball. Wrap in plastic wrap and place in plastic bag; refrigerate for at least 2 hours or until firm. *(Marzipan can be refrigerated for up to 2 weeks or frozen for longer storage.)* Makes 1 lb (500 g) or 2 cups (500 mL).

Per 1 tbsp (15 mL): about • 83 calories • 2 g protein • 5 g fat • 9 g carbohydrate

Black Bean Raisin Bread

The Atlantic Ocean isn't far away from LaHave Bakery in Lunenburg County, Nova Scotia, where this sturdy, wholesome loaf originates. For some, beans are a surprise ingredient in bread, but since they add color, moisture and nutrients, they are a welcome addition.

Per slice: about
• 106 calories   • 4 g protein
• 1 g fat   • 21 g carbohydrate

1-1/2 cups	dried black beans	375 mL
1 cup	raisins	250 mL
1 tsp	granulated sugar	5 mL
1/4 cup	warm water	50 mL
1	pkg active dry yeast (or 1 tbsp/15 mL)	1
1/4 cup	fancy molasses	50 mL
2 tbsp	vegetable oil	25 mL
2 tsp	salt	10 mL
3 cups	whole wheat flour	750 mL
4 cups	(approx) all-purpose flour	1 L
1	egg	1
1 tbsp	water	15 mL

● In large saucepan, bring beans and 8 cups (2 L) cold water to boil. Reduce heat to medium-low; cover and simmer for about 1 hour or until tender. Drain, reserving cooking liquid. Purée beans.

● Combine raisins with 1/2 cup (125 mL) of the hot reserved cooking liquid; set aside. In small bowl, dissolve sugar in warm water. Sprinkle in yeast; let stand for 10 minutes or until frothy.

● In large bowl, whisk together 1-1/2 cups (375 mL) of the reserved cooking liquid, molasses, oil, undrained raisins, salt, beans and yeast mixture. With electric mixer, beat in whole wheat flour; beat for 2 minutes. With wooden spoon, gradually stir in enough of the all-purpose flour to make firm slightly sticky dough.

● Turn out dough onto lightly floured surface; knead for 10 to 12 minutes or until smooth and elastic, adding enough of the remaining flour as necessary. Place in greased bowl, turning to grease all over. Cover with plastic wrap; let rise until doubled in bulk, 1-1/2 to 2 hours.

● Punch down dough; turn out onto lightly floured surface. Divide into thirds. Shape each into round loaf, stretching dough down all around and tucking underneath to shape. Place on greased baking sheets; cover and let rise until doubled in bulk, about 45 minutes.

● Beat egg with water; brush over loaves. Bake in center of 375°F (190°C) oven for 45 to 50 minutes or until loaves sound hollow when tapped on bottom. Remove from pans; let cool on racks. Makes 3 loaves, 16 slices each.

Raisin Walnut Soda Bread

Soda bread is so easy you can stir it up in five minutes. This one features whole wheat flour.

Per wedge: about
• 222 calories   • 7 g protein
• 5 g fat   • 40 g carbohydrate
• high source of fiber

2 cups	whole wheat flour	500 mL
1 cup	(approx) all-purpose flour	250 mL
2/3 cup	raisins	150 mL
1/2 cup	coarsely chopped walnuts	125 mL
4 tsp	granulated sugar	20 mL
1 tsp	baking powder	5 mL
1 tsp	baking soda	5 mL
1 tsp	salt	5 mL
1-1/2 cups	buttermilk	375 mL

● In large bowl, stir together whole wheat and all-purpose flours, raisins, walnuts, sugar, baking powder, baking soda and salt. Make well in center; pour in buttermilk all at once and stir just until combined. Knead lightly into ball.

● Transfer dough to greased baking sheet; pat into round about 1 inch (2.5 cm) thick. With serrated knife, cut deep X across surface. Dust with more all-purpose flour. Bake in center of 400°F (200°C) oven for 30 to 35 minutes or until cake tester inserted in center comes out clean. Remove from pan; let cool on rack. Cut into wedges. Makes 1 loaf, 10 wedges.

Fruity Soda Bread ▲

4 cups	all-purpose flour	1 L
1/3 cup	each raisins, dried currants, mixed candied fruit and chopped dried figs	75 mL
3 tbsp	granulated sugar	50 mL
1 tbsp	baking powder	15 mL
1 tsp	baking soda	5 mL
1/2 tsp	salt	2 mL
1-3/4 cups	buttermilk	425 mL
3 tbsp	vegetable oil	50 mL
1	egg	1
1-1/2 tsp	grated orange rind	7 mL
	GLAZE	
1/2 cup	icing sugar	125 mL
1 tbsp	orange juice	15 mL

● In large bowl, stir together flour, raisins, currants, candied fruit, figs, sugar, baking powder, baking soda and salt. In separate bowl, whisk together buttermilk, oil, egg and orange rind; pour over dry ingredients and stir just until moistened.

● Turn out dough onto lightly floured surface; knead lightly 10 times or just until dough holds together. Place on greased baking sheet; flatten into 9-inch (23 cm) circle that is 3 inches (8 cm) thick. With serrated knife, score top into sixths. Bake in center of 350°F (180°C) oven for 45 to 50 minutes or until cake tester inserted in center comes out clean. Let cool on pan on rack for 5 minutes.

● GLAZE: Mix icing sugar with orange juice; spread over warm bread. Cut into wedges or slices. Makes 1 loaf, 20 wedges.

W*ith the use of white flour and the addition of dried and candied fruit, soda bread goes glamorous at the hands of our nutrition editor, Anne Lindsay. Try it for breakfast, brunch or teatime, especially if you have houseguests.*

Per wedge: about
- 173 calories
- 3 g fat
- 4 g protein
- 33 g carbohydrate

Barm Brack

From Larkin's Bake Shop & Café in Halifax comes this bestselling Irish bread made both at Halloween and Christmas.

Per slice: about
- 272 calories
- 6 g protein
- 4 g fat
- 54 g carbohydrate
- good source of iron

TIP: If loaf is browning too quickly during baking, cover lightly with foil.

1/3 cup	granulated sugar	75 mL
1-1/4 cups	warm milk	300 mL
1	pkg active dry yeast (or 1 tbsp/15 mL)	1
4-1/4 cups	(approx) all-purpose flour	1.05 L
1 tsp	salt	5 mL
1 tsp	each allspice, cinnamon and nutmeg	5 mL
1/4 cup	butter	50 mL
2	eggs, beaten	2
1-1/3 cups	raisins	325 mL
2/3 cup	dried currants	150 mL
2/3 cup	mixed candied peel	150 mL
1 tbsp	grated lemon rind	15 mL
	GLAZE	
2 tsp	liquid honey	10 mL
1 tbsp	boiling water	15 mL

● In small bowl, dissolve 1 tbsp (15 mL) of the sugar in warm milk. Sprinkle in yeast; let stand for 10 minutes or until frothy.

● In large bowl, stir together 3-3/4 cups (925 mL) of the flour, remaining sugar, salt, allspice, cinnamon and nutmeg. Using pastry blender or two knives, cut in butter until mixture forms fine crumbs. Add yeast mixture and eggs; stir until sticky dough forms.

● Turn out dough onto lightly floured surface. Knead for 5 to 10 minutes or until smooth and elastic, adding up to 1/2 cup (125 mL) more flour if necessary. Cover with tea towel; let rest for 5 minutes. Flatten dough into rectangle; sprinkle with half each of the raisins, currants, candied peel and rind. Roll up into cylinder; knead for 3 minutes. Repeat with remaining raisins, currants, peel and rind. Cover and let rise in warm draft-free place until doubled in bulk, 45 to 60 minutes.

● Punch down dough; shape into 8-inch (20 cm) circle and gently pat into greased 9-inch (1.5 L) round cake pan. Cover and let rise until just above top of pan, 30 to 45 minutes. Bake in center of 350°F (180°C) oven for 1 hour or until loaf sounds hollow when tapped on bottom. Remove from pan; let cool on rack until just warm.

● GLAZE: Stir honey with boiling water; brush over warm bread. Makes 1 loaf, 16 slices.

JUST HOW MUCH FLOUR?

The amount of flour in a recipe usually varies and this variation is often what scares off first-time bread makers. However, once you've had your hands on the dough, you'll quickly get to know when the dough is too wet and sticky and should have a little flour kneaded in.

● It's easy to do this while kneading: simply dust the kneading surface with flour and the dough will absorb it. If a dough is too dry and hard to knead, dribble additional liquid called for in the recipe and knead in on an unfloured surface (unless otherwise noted in the recipe).

● Unbleached or regular all-purpose flour (the flour called for in most of our recipes) can vary in protein content and moistness, and with these variations, slightly different amounts will be needed for the same recipes. This happens among national brands, with the same brand in different seasons of the year and with the age of the flour.

● Bread flour or flour with added gluten has a higher protein content and you need to add either slightly less flour or, if it's easier, slightly more liquid to the recipe. This is true for both handmade and bread machine recipes.

Walnut Bread

Pinch	granulated sugar	Pinch
1-1/2 cups	warm water	375 mL
2-1/2 tsp	active dry yeast	12 mL
1 tbsp	walnut or vegetable oil	15 mL
2-1/4 cups	all-purpose flour	550 mL
1 cup	whole wheat flour	250 mL
3/4 cup	rye flour	175 mL
1 tsp	salt	5 mL
1-1/2 cups	toasted chopped walnuts	375 mL
3/4 cup	raisins (optional)	175 mL
	Cornmeal	
1	egg, lightly beaten	1

● In large bowl, dissolve sugar in warm water. Sprinkle in yeast; let stand for 10 minutes or until frothy. Stir in oil. With wooden spoon, stir in all-purpose, whole wheat and rye flours and salt until shaggy soft dough forms.

● Turn out dough onto lightly floured surface; knead for 5 minutes or until smooth and elastic. Cover with tea towel; let rest for 5 minutes. Flatten into 12-inch (30 cm) disk.

● Sprinkle walnuts, and raisins (if using), over dough; fold edges into center to cover nuts, pinching to seal at center. Knead for about 3 minutes or until nuts are evenly distributed. Form into ball. Place in lightly greased bowl, turning to grease all over. Cover with plastic wrap; let rise in warm draft-free place until doubled in bulk, about 1 hour.

● Punch down dough; form into round loaf. Place on cornmeal-dusted baking sheet. Cover with damp tea towel; let rise until doubled in bulk, about 45 minutes.

● Brush loaf with egg. With serrated knife, cut crisscross pattern on top. Bake in center of 400°F (200°C) oven for 40 minutes or until loaf sounds hollow when tapped on bottom. Makes 1 large loaf, 16 slices.

*W*alnut bread is the finest partner a cheese could ever ask for. Its rye and whole wheat flours, plus the crunchy bite of the nuts, go spectacularly well with Brie, crumbly old Cheddar, Gouda or a luscious blue cheese.

Per slice: about
- 198 calories
- 9 g fat
- 6 g protein
- 25 g carbohydrate

Quick Corn Bread

1 cup	cornmeal	250 mL
1 cup	all-purpose flour	250 mL
1 tbsp	baking powder	15 mL
1/2 tsp	salt	2 mL
1/4 tsp	pepper	1 mL
3/4 cup	2% cottage cheese	175 mL
2 tbsp	butter, softened	25 mL
2	eggs	2
2 tbsp	granulated sugar	25 mL
1 cup	cooked or thawed corn kernels	250 mL
1/3 cup	diced sweet red pepper	75 mL

● Grease 9-inch (23 cm) pie plate; sprinkle with 1 tbsp (15 mL) of the cornmeal. Set aside.

● In large bowl, stir together all-purpose flour, baking powder, salt and pepper; set aside.

● In food processor or blender, purée cottage cheese; scrape into another bowl. Stir in remaining cornmeal; let stand for 10 minutes. Using electric mixer, beat in butter until fluffy; beat in eggs and sugar. Pour over dry ingredients. Sprinkle with corn and red pepper; stir just until dry ingredients are moistened.

● Mound batter into prepared pie plate, leaving 1-inch (2.5 cm) border. Bake in center of 350°F (180°C) oven for about 45 minutes or until cake tester inserted in center comes out clean. Let cool slightly in pan on rack; cut into wedges. Serve warm or at room temperature. Makes 6 servings.

*W*hen Canadians think of corn bread, they think of a baking-powder quickbread baked in a loaf or cake pan. Here's a lighter version where naturally low-in-fat cottage cheese replaces some of the oil and butter of a traditional corn bread.

Per serving: about
- 294 calories
- 7 g fat
- 11 g protein
- 47 g carbohydrate

Reuben Sandwich Loaf ▶

This dark, caraway-scented loaf is truly delicious baked with its savory reuben sandwich filling — smoked meat, Swiss cheese and sauerkraut. Or, shape into baguettes; the recipe makes three.

Per serving: about
- 364 calories
- 13 g fat
- very high source of fiber
- excellent source of iron
- 16 g protein
- 48 g carbohydrate
- good source of calcium

TIP: You can make the loaf ahead. Slice and freeze, then defrost and heat up as much as you need at a time.

1 cup	water	250 mL
1/4 cup	fancy molasses	50 mL
2 tbsp	shortening	25 mL
1-1/2 cups	dark rye flour	375 mL
1-1/4 cups	(approx) all-purpose flour	300 mL
1/2 cup	whole wheat flour	125 mL
2 tbsp	unsweetened cocoa powder	25 mL
1 tbsp	each caraway and flax seeds	15 mL
1-1/2 tsp	quick-rising (instant) dry yeast	7 mL
1 tsp	granulated sugar	5 mL
1 tsp	salt	5 mL
	FILLING	
2 tbsp	grainy or regular Dijon mustard	25 mL
6	thick slices smoked meat or pastrami (about 6 oz/175 g)	6
1 cup	sauerkraut, rinsed and squeezed dry	250 mL
4 oz	Swiss cheese, shredded	125 g
	GLAZE	
1	egg white, beaten	1
1 tsp	caraway seeds	15 mL

● In small saucepan, heat together water, molasses and shortening until at 120°F (50°C); stir until shortening is melted. In large bowl, stir together rye flour, 1/2 cup (125 mL) of the all-purpose flour, the whole wheat flour, cocoa, caraway seeds, flax seeds, yeast, sugar and salt. Stir in shortening mixture. With wooden spoon, gradually stir in enough of the remaining flour to make soft dough, mixing with hands if necessary.

● Turn out dough onto lightly floured surface; knead for 8 to 10 minutes or until smooth and elastic. Place in greased bowl, turning to grease all over. Cover with plastic wrap; let rise in warm draft-free place until doubled in bulk, 30 to 60 minutes.

● Punch down dough; turn out onto lightly floured surface. Roll out into 14- x 12-inch (35 x 30 cm) rectangle. Place on greased baking sheet.

● FILLING: Spread mustard lengthwise in 3-inch (8 cm) strip along center of rectangle, leaving 1-inch (2.5 cm) border uncovered at ends. Top mustard with 2 layers each meat, sauerkraut and cheese.

● Starting at corner of dough, make diagonal cuts 1 inch (2.5 cm) apart almost to filling along one long side of dough. Repeat on other side in opposite direction. Alternating strips from each side, fold strips over filling to resemble braid, overlapping ends by 1 inch (2.5 cm).

● GLAZE: Brush with egg white to seal. Cover and let rise in warm draft-free place until doubled in bulk, 30 to 40 minutes. Brush top with remaining egg white; sprinkle with caraway seeds.

● Bake in center of 350°F (180°C) oven for 30 to 40 minutes or until puffed and dark brown. Remove from pan; let cool slightly on rack. Serve warm or let cool completely. Makes 8 servings, 16 slices.

BREAD MACHINE METHOD
(for dough only)
● Into pan of 2 lb (1 kg) machine, add (in order) water, molasses, shortening, sugar, salt, dark rye flour, all-purpose flour, whole wheat flour, cocoa, caraway seeds, flax seeds and yeast. (Do not let yeast touch liquid.) Choose dough setting; shape and bake as directed.

Stuffed Cheese and Onion Pinwheel

A *golden swirl of Cheddar, ham and caramelized onions turns this loaf into a spectacular addition to any entertaining buffet — be it for brunch, lunch or supper.*

Per slice: about
- 103 calories
- 4 g protein
- 3 g fat
- 15 g carbohydrate

1 tsp	granulated sugar	5 mL
1/2 cup	warm water	125 mL
1-1/2 tsp	quick-rising (instant) dry yeast	7 mL
1/4 cup	milk	50 mL
1/4 cup	plain yogurt	50 mL
2-1/2 cups	all-purpose flour	625 mL
1 tsp	salt	5 mL
	FILLING	
1 tbsp	olive oil	15 mL
1/3 cup	cubed Black Forest ham (2 oz/50 g)	75 mL
2 tsp	butter	10 mL
3 cups	thinly sliced onions	750 mL
1-1/2 tsp	cider vinegar	7 mL
2/3 cup	shredded Cheddar cheese	150 mL
	GLAZE	
1	egg	1
1/4 cup	water	50 mL

● In large bowl, dissolve sugar in warm water. Sprinkle in yeast; let stand for 10 minutes or until frothy. Stir in milk and yogurt. With electric mixer, beat in 1-1/2 cups (375 mL) of the flour and salt, beating for 3 minutes. With wooden spoon, stir in remaining flour until dough comes away from side of bowl.

● Turn out dough onto lightly floured surface. Knead for about 5 minutes or until smooth and elastic. Place in greased bowl, turning to grease all over. Cover with plastic wrap; let rise in warm draft-free place until doubled in bulk, about 1-1/2 hours.

● FILLING: Meanwhile, in large skillet, heat 1 tsp (5 mL) of the oil over medium-high heat; cook ham for 2 minutes or until golden at edges and beginning to crisp. Transfer to bowl and set aside. Add remaining oil and butter to skillet; cook onions over low heat, stirring occasionally, for 20 to 25 minutes or until golden and sweet. Add vinegar; cook for 5 minutes. Stir into ham in bowl; let cool to room temperature.

● Punch down dough; turn out onto lightly floured surface. Knead into ball; divide in half. Roll or press out each half into 10- x 6-inch (25 x 15 cm) rectangle. With long side horizontal, spread with half of the filling, leaving 1/2-inch (1 cm) border uncovered at sides and bottom. Sprinkle filling with 1/3 cup (75 mL) of the Cheddar.

● Starting at top, roll into cylinder; pinch along seam to smooth and seal. Fold in ends to meet seam; pinch to seal. Place, seam side down, on half of lightly greased baking sheet. Repeat with remaining dough; place on other half of baking sheet. Cover and let rise until doubled in bulk, about 1 hour.

● GLAZE: Whisk egg with water; brush over loaves. With serrated knife, make one shallow slash lengthwise down center of each loaf, being careful not to cut into filling. Bake in center of 400°F (200°C) oven for 20 minutes or until golden brown and loaves sound hollow when tapped on bottom. Remove from pan; let cool slightly on rack. Serve warm or let cool completely. Makes 2 small loaves, 10 slices each.

BREAD MACHINE METHOD
(for dough only)
● Increase flour to 3 cups (750 mL). Into pan of machine, add (in order) water, milk, yogurt, salt, sugar, flour and yeast. (Do not let yeast touch liquid.) Choose dough setting; shape and bake as directed.

Braided Cheese Bread

1 tbsp	granulated sugar	15 mL
1 cup	warm water	250 mL
1	pkg active dry yeast (or 1 tbsp/15 mL)	1
2	eggs, lightly beaten	2
4 cups	(approx) all-purpose flour	1 L
2 tbsp	vegetable oil	25 mL
1 tsp	salt	5 mL
	FILLING	
3 tbsp	Dijon mustard	50 mL
1-3/4 cups	(approx) freshly grated Parmesan cheese	425 mL

● In large bowl, dissolve sugar in warm water. Sprinkle in yeast; let stand for 10 minutes or until frothy. Reserve 1 tbsp (15 mL) of the eggs for glaze. With electric mixer, beat remaining eggs into yeast mixture along with 2 cups (500 mL) of the flour, oil and salt. With wooden spoon, gradually beat in enough of the remaining flour to make stiff dough.

● Turn out dough onto lightly floured surface. Knead for 8 to 10 minutes or until smooth and elastic. Place in greased bowl, turning to grease all over. Cover with plastic wrap; let rise in warm draft-free place until doubled in bulk, about 1 hour.

● Punch down dough; turn out onto lightly floured surface. Knead into ball; divide into thirds. Divide each into 3 pieces. Roll each piece into 10- x 5-inch (25 x 12 cm) rectangle.

● FILLING: Spread each rectangle with 1 tsp (5 mL) of the mustard; sprinkle with about 3 tbsp (50 mL) Parmesan cheese.

● Starting at long edge, roll up each rectangle tightly to form rope, pinching seam and ends to seal. (Ropes should be same length.) Braid 3 ropes together, pinching ends to seal together; tuck ends under. Repeat with remaining dough. Place on greased baking sheets. Cover and let rise until doubled in bulk, about 45 minutes.

● Mix reserved egg with 1 tbsp (15 mL) water; brush over braids. Bake in center of 375°F (190°C) oven for 20 minutes or until golden brown and loaves sound hollow when tapped on bottom. Remove from pans; let cool on racks. Makes 3 loaves, 6 slices each.

T*he best cheeses to add to bread are the most strongly flavored ones. Naturally aged Parmesan (marked* Parmigiano Reggiano *on the* rind) *is the cheese of choice.*

Per slice: about
- 173 calories
- 8 g protein
- 5 g fat
- 23 g carbohydrate

Italian Herb Bread Machine Mix

3-1/4 cups	all-purpose flour	800 mL
2 tbsp	granulated sugar	25 mL
1 tbsp	skim milk powder	15 mL
1-1/2 tsp	salt	7 mL
1 tsp	each dried oregano and basil	5 mL
1-1/2 tsp	quick-rising (instant) dry yeast (or 1-1/4 tsp/6 mL bread machine yeast)	7 mL

● In large bowl, combine flour, sugar, skim milk powder, salt, oregano and basil. Spoon into decorative bag and seal. Wrap yeast in small bag or plastic wrap; attach to flour mixture. *(Mix and yeast can be stored at room temperature for up to 3 days or refrigerated for up to 1 month.)* Makes 1 package, enough for 1 loaf.

BREAD MACHINE ITALIAN HERB LOAF
● Into pan of 1-1/2 to 2 lb (750 g to 1 kg) bread machine, add (in order) 1-1/4 cups (300 mL) water, 2 tbsp (25 mL) vegetable oil, 3 tbsp (50 mL) freshly grated Parmesan cheese, Italian Herb Bread Machine Mix and yeast. (Do not let yeast touch liquid.) Choose basic setting. Let baked loaf cool on rack. Makes 1 loaf, 12 slices.

H*ere's a great recipe from* Canadian Living's *Heather Howe. Make it up for your contributions to a festive bake sale or bazaar, or for much appreciated hostess gifts all year round.*

Per slice: about
- 161 calories
- 4 g protein
- 3 g fat
- 28 g carbohydrate

Caraway Beer Quick Loaf ▲

*B*eer lends its yeasty flavor
to a loaf raised with baking
powder and baking soda.
Toast any leftover slices and
spread with cream cheese.

Per slice: about
- 228 calories
- 5 g fat
- 6 g protein
- 38 g carbohydrate

4 cups	all-purpose flour	1 L
1/4 cup	granulated sugar	50 mL
1 tbsp	baking powder	15 mL
1-1/2 tsp	salt	7 mL
1 tsp	baking soda	5 mL
1/4 cup	butter	50 mL
4 tsp	caraway seeds	20 mL
2	eggs	2
3/4 cup	buttermilk	175 mL
3/4 cup	beer	175 mL

● In large bowl, stir together flour, sugar, baking powder, salt and baking soda. With pastry blender or two knives, cut in butter until mixture resembles fine crumbs. Stir in caraway seeds. In separate bowl, beat together eggs, buttermilk and beer; add to flour mixture all at once, stirring with fork to make soft dough.

● Turn out dough onto lightly floured surface; knead lightly about 10 times. Shape dough into oval to fit into greased 9- x 5-inch (2 L) loaf pan. With serrated knife, cut shallow slash lengthwise down center. Bake in center of 350°F (180°C) oven for 1 to 1-1/4 hours or until golden brown and cake tester inserted in center comes out clean. Remove from pan; let cool on rack. Makes 1 loaf, 12 slices.

Mediterranean Stuffed Bread

1 cup	warm water	250 mL
1 tbsp	liquid honey	15 mL
2 tsp	active or quick-rising (instant) dry yeast	10 mL
2-1/2 cups	(approx) all-purpose flour	625 mL
2 tbsp	semolina or cornmeal	25 mL
2 tbsp	olive oil	25 mL
1-1/4 tsp	salt	6 mL
	FILLING	
16	dry-packed sun-dried tomato halves	16
3/4 cup	crumbled feta cheese	175 mL
1/2 cup	chopped pitted black olives	125 mL
1/4 cup	minced fresh parsley	50 mL
1/4 cup	minced green onions	50 mL
3	cloves garlic, minced	3
3 tbsp	olive oil	50 mL
1/2 tsp	each dried oregano and basil	2 mL
1/4 tsp	each salt and pepper	1 mL
	TOPPING	
2 tbsp	semolina or cornmeal	25 mL
1 tbsp	olive oil	15 mL
1 tbsp	chopped fresh parsley	15 mL

● In large bowl, whisk warm water with honey. Sprinkle in yeast; let stand for 10 minutes or until frothy. With wooden spoon, stir in 2-1/4 cups (550 mL) of the flour, semolina, oil and salt until dough comes away from side of bowl.

● Turn out dough onto lightly floured surface. Knead for 8 to 10 minutes or until soft and slightly sticky, dusting with remaining flour as needed. Place in greased bowl, turning to grease all over. Cover with plastic wrap; let rise in warm draft-free place until doubled in bulk, about 45 minutes.

● FILLING: Meanwhile, in small bowl, cover sun-dried tomatoes with boiling water; let stand for 10 minutes or until softened. Drain and chop to make about 3/4 cup (175 mL). In bowl, toss together sun-dried tomatoes, cheese, black olives, parsley, onions, garlic, oil, oregano, basil, salt and pepper.

● Turn out dough onto lightly floured surface; roll out into 16- x 9-inch (40 x 23 cm) rectangle. Spread with filling. Starting at long side, roll up into cylinder; pinch along seam to smooth and seal. Flatten slightly; pinch ends to seal.

● TOPPING: Sprinkle semolina on baking sheet; place loaf on top. Brush with oil; sprinkle with parsley and pat lightly into dough. Cover and let rise until doubled in bulk, about 45 minutes.

● Bake on lowest rack in 375°F (190°C) oven for 35 minutes or until well-browned and loaf sounds hollow when tapped on bottom. Remove from pan. Let cool slightly on rack. Serve warm or cold. Makes 1 loaf, 18 slices.

VARIATION

● GRILLED MEDITERRANEAN STUFFED BREAD: To grill on the barbecue, stack two rimless baking sheets; line top with foil or parchment paper. Follow recipe, then place baking sheets with loaf on grill over medium-high heat; close lid and reduce heat to medium-low. Grill for 30 to 40 minutes or until well-browned and loaf sounds hollow when tapped on bottom.

Montrealer Marcy Goldman, a professional baker and consultant, created a series of summer picnic and party loaves to bake in the oven or on the barbecue. This zesty, chock-full loaf can be served at room temperature as an appetizer or warm with salad to make a meal.

Per slice: about
- 140 calories
- 6 g fat
- 3 g protein
- 18 g carbohydrate

Buns, Rolls & Bagels

Little breads — some savory, some sweet — guarantee more crust and more chew. How can anyone resist the aroma of freshly baked bagels, crunchy break-apart-and-nibble breadsticks, tender oatmeal rolls and, of course, cinnamon buns — the sweet sirens of the bread world.

Montreal-Style Bagels ▶

Here's how to make authentic Montreal-style bagels at home, including instructions for the unique hot-water dunking that makes a bagel a bagel and not just a round bun with a hole in the center.

Per bagel: about
- 208 calories
- 6 g fat
- good source of iron
- 7 g protein
- 32 g carbohydrate

TIPS
● Unless the ends of the dough are pinched together very firmly, they will come apart in the water.
● The bagels can be individually wrapped in plastic wrap and frozen in a rigid airtight container for up to 2 weeks.

1 tsp	granulated sugar	5 mL
1 cup	warm water	250 mL
1	pkg active dry yeast (or 1 tbsp/15 mL)	1
2	eggs	2
1 tbsp	vegetable oil	15 mL
3-1/2 cups	(approx) all-purpose flour	875 mL
2 tbsp	granulated sugar	25 mL
2 tsp	salt	10 mL
	POACHING LIQUID	
16 cups	water	4 L
2 tbsp	granulated sugar	25 mL
	GLAZE	
1/2 cup	sesame or poppy seeds	125 mL
1	egg, beaten	1

● In large bowl, dissolve 1 tsp (5 mL) sugar in warm water. Sprinkle in yeast; let stand for 10 minutes or until frothy. Whisk in eggs and oil. Beat in 2 cups (500 mL) of the flour, 2 tbsp (25 mL) sugar and salt until smooth. With wooden spoon, gradually stir in enough of the remaining flour to make soft but not sticky dough.

● Turn out dough onto lightly floured surface; knead for 8 to 10 minutes or until smooth and elastic. Place in greased bowl, turning to grease all over. Cover with plastic wrap; let rise in warm draft-free place until doubled in bulk, 1 to 1-1/2 hours.

● Punch down dough; turn out onto lightly floured surface. Knead several times. Divide into 12 pieces; roll each into 12-inch (30 cm) rope, covering ropes with tea towel as you work.

● For each rope, bring ends of dough together, overlapping by about 1 inch (2.5 cm) and stretching overlap around other end to meet underneath; pinch firmly to seal. Place on lightly floured baking sheet; cover and let rise in warm draft-free place for 15 minutes.

● POACHING LIQUID: In wide saucepan, bring water to boil; add sugar. Reduce heat to medium. Slip bagels into water, 3 or 4 at a time; cook for 1 minute. Turn with slotted spatula; cook for 1 minute. Using spatula, transfer bagels to greased baking sheets.

● GLAZE: Place sesame seeds on plate. Brush egg over bagels. One at a time, dip egg side into seeds; return to baking sheet. Bake in center of 400°F (200°C) oven for 20 to 25 minutes or until golden and bagels sound hollow when tapped on bottom. Remove from pan; let cool on racks. Makes 12 bagels.

Good and Grainy Rolls or Bread

Your choice. A healthy loaf for sandwiches, toast or croutons — or rolls to slice and fill with chicken or egg salad, roasted vegetables and hummus or whatever catches your fancy.

Per roll: about
- 163 calories
- 4 g fat
- 5 g protein
- 29 g carbohydrate

1 cup	water	250 mL
2 tbsp	shortening	25 mL
2 tbsp	maple syrup or liquid honey	25 mL
1-1/3 cups	(approx) all-purpose flour	325 mL
1 cup	whole wheat flour	250 mL
1/2 cup	quick-cooking rolled oats	125 mL
1/4 cup	natural bran	50 mL
3 tbsp	skim milk powder	50 mL
1 tbsp	flax seeds	15 mL
1-1/2 tsp	salt	7 mL
1-1/2 tsp	quick-rising (instant) dry yeast	7 mL

● In small saucepan, heat together water, shortening and maple syrup until at 120°F (50°C) and shortening is melted. In large bowl, stir together 3/4 cup (175 mL) of the all-purpose flour, the whole wheat flour, rolled oats, bran, skim milk powder, flax seeds, salt and yeast; stir in shortening mixture. With wooden spoon, gradually stir in enough of the remaining flour to make soft dough, mixing with hands if necessary.

● Turn out dough onto lightly floured surface. Knead for 8 to 10 minutes or until smooth and elastic. Place in greased bowl, turning to grease all over. Cover with plastic wrap; let rise in warm draft-free place until doubled in bulk, 30 to 60 minutes.

● Punch down dough; turn out onto lightly floured surface. Shape as desired into rolls or loaf. For rolls, shape dough into log; divide into 10 pieces. Shape each into ball, stretching and pinching dough underneath to make tops smooth. Place about 2 inches (5 cm) apart on greased baking sheet. For loaf, gently pull dough into 11- x 8-inch (28 x 20 cm) rectangle. Starting at narrow end, roll up into cylinder; pinch along seam to smooth and seal. Fit into greased 8- x 4-inch (1.5 L) loaf pan. Cover and let rise in warm draft-free place until doubled in bulk, 30 to 60 minutes.

● Bake in center of 375°F (190°C) oven for 20 minutes for rolls, 40 to 50 minutes for loaf, or until browned and rolls, or loaf, sound hollow when tapped on bottom. (For crisp crust on loaf, remove from pan and bake for 5 minutes longer.) Remove from pan; let cool on rack. Makes 10 rolls or 1 loaf, 10 slices.

BREAD MACHINE METHOD
● FOR ROLLS (for dough only): Into pan of 2 lb (1 kg) bread machine, add (in order) water, shortening, maple syrup, salt, all-purpose flour, whole wheat flour, rolled oats, bran, milk powder, flax seeds and yeast. (Do not let yeast touch liquid.) Choose dough setting, then turn out onto lightly floured surface and knead several times. Shape into rolls and bake as directed.

● FOR LOAF: Into pan of 2 lb (1 kg) bread machine, add (in order) water, shortening, maple syrup, salt, all-purpose flour, whole wheat flour, rolled oats, bran, milk powder, flax seeds and yeast. (Do not let yeast touch liquid.) Choose basic setting. Let baked loaf cool on rack. Makes 1 loaf.

SURFACE SLASHES

Add a decorative touch to loaves or rolls with surface slashes.

● Use a very fine sharp serrated knife or other thin-bladed sharp knife to gently cut into the surface of a risen loaf just before it goes into the oven.

● For a long loaf in a bread pan, cut lengthwise slash or slash diagonally as for baguettes. For round loaves, cut either a shallow cross or three intersecting slashes. As the bread rises, the slashes expand into a cross, crown or star shape. Other popular finishes include a crisscross pattern, parallel cuts or short random cuts.

● Dusting the loaves with flour after baking or applying a glaze beforehand accentuates the slashes.

FOR GOOD MEASURE

Careful measuring of ingredients is important for best results when baking. Also, be sure you consistently follow either the imperial or the metric system throughout the recipe — never a combination of the two.
● There are two types of measuring cups: dry-ingredient and liquid-ingredient. Dry-ingredient measures come in sets of graduated sizes in imperial (1/4 cup, 1/3 cup, 1/2 cup and 1 cup) and metric (50 mL, 75 mL, 125 mL, 250 mL).

Levels are marked on the outside of liquid-ingredient measures, with enough space below the rim to prevent spills.
● Measuring spoons are used for both dry and liquid ingredients. Imperial measures are 1/4 tsp, 1/2 tsp, 1 tsp, 1 tbsp; metric measures are 1 mL, 2 mL, 5 mL, 15 mL.

Dry Ingredients
● Lightly spoon dry ingredients into dry measure, filling until heaping. Level off by running straight edge of

knife across top. Do not pack or tap measure when filling. (If flour is packed, you could end up with 1/4 cup/50 mL more than called for.) Brown sugar, however, should be packed lightly until it holds the shape of the measure when it is turned out.

Liquid Ingredients
● Place liquid measure on counter; pour in liquid to desired level, bending down to check measurement at eye level and pouring out or adding as necessary.

Fat Ingredients
● For soft fats, press firmly into dry measure, then level off top. For butter and other firm fats, use handy package markings as guides to slice off the amount needed. When there are no markings, use the displacement method: If a recipe calls for 1/2 cup (125 mL) butter, fill liquid measuring cup with 1/2 cup (125 mL) water; submerge enough butter to make water level rise to 1 cup (250 mL). Drain off water.

Nova Scotia Oatmeal Buns

1/2 cup	packed brown sugar	125 mL
1/2 cup	warm water	125 mL
2	pkg active dry yeast (or 2 tbsp/25 mL)	2
1-1/4 cups	boiling water	300 mL
1 cup	quick-cooking rolled oats	250 mL
1/3 cup	butter, softened	75 mL
1-1/2 tsp	salt	7 mL
2	eggs, lightly beaten	2
4-1/2 cups	(approx) all-purpose flour	1.125 L
1 cup	whole wheat flour	250 mL
	TOPPING	
1	egg, lightly beaten	1
1/4 cup	quick-cooking rolled oats	50 mL

● In small bowl, dissolve 1 tsp (5 mL) of the sugar in warm water. Sprinkle in yeast; let stand for 10 minutes or until frothy. Meanwhile, in large bowl, stir together boiling water, rolled oats, remaining sugar, butter and salt, stirring until sugar is dissolved and butter is melted. Let cool to lukewarm.

● Stir in yeast mixture and eggs. With electric mixer, beat in 2 cups (500 mL) of the all-purpose flour and whole wheat flour. With wooden spoon, stir in enough of the remaining flour to make soft dough.

● Turn out dough onto lightly floured surface; knead for 8 to 10 minutes or until smooth and elastic. Place in greased bowl, turning to grease all over. Cover with plastic wrap; let rise in warm draft-free place until doubled in bulk, about 1 hour.

● Punch down dough; turn out onto lightly floured surface. Divide into 12 portions. Shape each into ball, stretching and pinching dough underneath to make tops smooth. Place 2 inches (5 cm) apart on greased baking sheets. Cover and let rise in warm draft-free place until doubled in bulk, 30 to 45 minutes.

● TOPPING: Brush buns with egg; sprinkle with rolled oats. Bake in center of 375°F (190°C) oven for 30 minutes or until buns sound hollow when tapped on bottom. Remove from pans; let cool on racks. Makes 12 buns.

Nova Scotia is rightly proud of its tender, slightly nutty oatmeal buns.

Per bun: about
● 340 calories
● 8 g fat
● high source of fiber
● 10 g protein
● 58 g carbohydrate
● good source of iron

Caramelized Onion and Pepper Pinwheels ◀

3/4 cup	water	175 mL
2 tbsp	extra virgin olive oil	25 mL
2-1/4 cups	(approx) all-purpose flour	550 mL
1/4 cup	freshly grated Parmesan cheese	50 mL
1 tbsp	granulated sugar	15 mL
1-1/4 tsp	quick-rising (instant) dry yeast	6 mL
1 tsp	dried oregano or basil	5 mL
1 tsp	salt	5 mL
	FILLING	
3 tbsp	extra virgin olive oil	50 mL
2 cups	chopped onions	500 mL
3 tbsp	chopped fresh parsley	50 mL
1 tbsp	chopped fresh basil (or 1 tsp/5 mL dried)	15 mL
Pinch	each salt and pepper	Pinch
1	each sweet red and yellow pepper	1
1	large clove garlic, minced	1
1/2 cup	freshly grated Parmesan cheese	125 mL

● FILLING: In large skillet, heat 2 tbsp (25 mL) of the oil over low heat; cook onions, stirring often, for about 45 minutes or until very soft, sweet and golden. Stir in parsley, basil, salt and pepper. Let cool.

● Meanwhile, place red and yellow peppers on baking sheet; broil, turning often, for about 15 minutes or until blackened all over. Let cool. Peel off charred skin; seed, chop and add to onion mixture. *(Filling can be prepared to this point and refrigerated in airtight container for up to 24 hours.)* Stir in garlic. Set aside.

● In small saucepan, heat water with oil, stirring occasionally, until at 120°F (50°C). In large bowl, stir together 2 cups (500 mL) of the flour, Parmesan cheese, sugar, yeast, oregano and salt; stir in water mixture. With wooden spoon, gradually stir in enough of the remaining flour to make soft dough, mixing with hands if necessary.

● Turn out dough onto lightly floured surface; knead for about 8 minutes or until smooth and elastic. Place in greased bowl, turning to grease all over. Cover with plastic wrap; let rise in warm draft-free place until doubled in bulk, 30 to 60 minutes.

● Punch down dough; turn out onto lightly floured surface. Roll out into 24- x 8-inch (60 x 20 cm) rectangle. Brush with remaining 1 tbsp (15 mL) oil; sprinkle with Parmesan cheese. Sprinkle filling evenly over top. Starting at long side, roll up tightly, pinching seam to seal. With serrated knife, cut into 24 slices; arrange, cut side down, in greased 13- x 9-inch (3.5 L) cake pan. Cover and let rise in warm draft-free place until doubled in bulk, about 45 minutes.

● Bake in center of 375°F (190°C) oven for about 30 minutes or until top is golden and center is firm. Let cool in pan on rack for 5 minutes. Remove from pan; serve warm or let cool on rack. Makes 24 rolls.

BREAD MACHINE METHOD (for dough only)
● Into pan of 2 lb (1 kg) bread machine, add (in order) water, oil, salt, sugar, flour, Parmesan, oregano and yeast. (Do not let yeast touch liquid.) Choose dough setting. Remove from machine; shape and bake as directed.

S*tart with the heavenly aroma of onions slowly turning golden in a skillet as peppers roast in the oven, then finish with the delicious taste of these colorful swirled rolls. They add a magic touch to any brunch or dinner menu.*

Per roll: about
- 92 calories
- 4 g fat
- 3 g protein
- 12 g carbohydrate

Gunn's Cheese-Onion Buns

Winnipeg is home to one of the best bakeries in Canada — Gunn's, a three-generation, family-run business in the city's North End. Sheer deliciousness characterizes its breads and pastries, as these voluptuous cheese and poppy seed-swirled, onion-topped buns attest.

Per bun: about
- 354 calories
- 17 g fat
- good source of calcium and iron
- 11 g protein
- 39 g carbohydrate

2 tbsp	granulated sugar	25 mL
2 cups	warm milk	500 mL
1	pkg active dry yeast (or 1 tbsp/15 mL)	1
1/3 cup	granulated sugar	75 mL
3	eggs	3
1/3 cup	vegetable oil	75 mL
2 tsp	salt	10 mL
6-1/2 cups	(approx) all-purpose flour	1.625 L
2 tbsp	butter, melted	25 mL
3 cups	shredded old Cheddar cheese	750 mL
1/4 cup	poppy seeds	50 mL
2	onions, sliced	2
1/2 cup	(approx) mayonnaise	125 mL

● In small bowl, dissolve 2 tbsp (25 mL) sugar in warm milk. Sprinkle in yeast; let stand for 10 minutes or until frothy.

● Meanwhile, in large bowl and using electric mixer, beat together 1/3 cup (75 mL) sugar and 2 of the eggs for 7 minutes or until thick and pale yellow. Stir in yeast mixture, oil and salt. With wooden spoon, stir in enough of the flour to make firm, slightly sticky dough.

● Turn out dough onto lightly floured surface; knead for 10 to 12 minutes or until smooth and elastic, adding flour as necessary. Place in greased bowl, turning to grease all over. Cover with plastic wrap; let rise in warm draft-free place until doubled in bulk, about 2 hours.

● Punch down dough; turn out onto lightly floured surface. Knead into ball. Divide in half. Roll out each half into 16- x 12-inch (40 x 30 cm) rectangle. Brush each with half of the melted butter, leaving 1/2-inch (1 cm) border uncovered; sprinkle each with half of the cheese and poppy seeds. Beat remaining egg; brush some lightly over long edges.

● Starting at long side, roll up tightly; pinch seam to seal. Cut into 3/4-inch (2 cm) thick slices; place about 2 inches (5 cm) apart on greased baking sheet. Cover and let rise in warm draft-free place until doubled in bulk, 1-1/2 to 2 hours.

● Brush lightly with remaining egg; sprinkle with sliced onions. Top each with 1 tsp (5 mL) mayonnaise. Bake in 375°F (190°C) oven for 25 to 30 minutes or until golden brown and buns sound hollow when tapped on bottom. Remove from pan; let cool on racks. Makes 20 buns.

BREADSTICKS

● In large bowl, dissolve 2 tsp (10 mL) granulated sugar in 1/4 cup (50 mL) warm water. Sprinkle in 2 tsp (10 mL) active dry yeast; let stand for 10 minutes or until frothy.

● Stir in 1-1/4 cups (300 mL) warm water and 3 tbsp (50 mL) olive oil. With wooden spoon, stir in 4-1/2 cups (1.125 L) all-purpose flour and 2 tsp (10 mL) salt until shaggy dough forms.

● Turn out dough onto lightly floured surface; knead for about 8 minutes or until smooth and elastic. Place in greased bowl, turning to grease all over. Cover with plastic wrap; let rise in warm draft-free place until doubled in bulk, about 1-1/2 hours.

● Punch down dough; turn out onto lightly floured surface. Divide in half; pat each into 8- x 4-inch (20 x 10 cm) rectangle. Cover with tea towel; let rest for 10 minutes.

● Cut 1 rectangle crosswise into 16 strips. Holding at each end, gently pull each into 14-inch (35 cm) length. Place on two greased baking sheets; brush with 1-1/2 tsp (7 mL) olive oil. Let rest for 5 minutes.

● Bake in 450°F (230°C) oven for 15 minutes or until golden brown, rotating sheets halfway through. Transfer to racks to let cool. Repeat with remaining dough. Makes 32 pieces.

Per piece: about ● 81 calories ● 2 g protein ● 2 g fat ● 14 g carbohydrate

FINISHING TOUCHES

Glossy? Crusty? Golden? Tender? Here's how to give your loaf some of these special finishes. Except for the Tender-Soft, all finishes are added just before bread is put into the oven. Since risen bread is delicate, remember to brush, sprinkle or spray gently.

Glossy

For a matte shine, brush loaves with either milk or light cream. A shinier surface comes from a beaten whole egg, yolk or white — with the glossiest from the white, and the most golden from the yolk.

Crusty for the Big Chew

Spray loaves with water just before they go into the oven. Quickly spray a few times more during the first 5 to 10 minutes of baking.

A Sprinkle of Seeds

Brush loaves with milk, cream, a beaten egg, yolk or white. Sprinkle lightly with poppy or sesame seeds, sunflower seeds or pepitas (green pumpkin seeds).

Dusty Flour

Sieve flour over bread. Do not use with other finishes or the surface will become gummy.

Sparkle Aplenty

For sweet breads or rolls, brush tops with milk or cream and sprinkle with granulated sugar (the coarser, the better).

From the Granary

Brush tops of loaves with milk, cream, a beaten egg, yolk or white or with water. Sprinkle lightly with rolled oats, flaked wheat or barley, cracked wheat, bran, wheat germ or any other grains.

Tender-Soft

Brush or gently rub top of bread with butter as soon as it comes out of the oven. Note that bread coming out of the oven has a harder crust than when it cools. To soften the crust even more, cover bread lightly with a clean tea towel as it cools.

Old-Fashioned Mashed Potato Rolls

1-1/4 cups	milk	300 mL
1/2 cup	mashed potato	125 mL
1/2 cup	shortening	125 mL
4-1/2 cups	(approx) all-purpose flour	1.125 L
1/4 cup	granulated sugar	50 mL
2 tsp	quick-rising (instant) dry yeast	10 mL
1-1/2 tsp	salt	7 mL
1	egg, lightly beaten	1
2 tbsp	butter, melted (optional)	25 mL

● In small saucepan, heat together milk, potato and shortening until at 120°F (50°C) and shortening is melted. In large bowl, stir together 3-1/2 cups (875 mL) of the flour, sugar, yeast and salt; stir in milk mixture and egg. With wooden spoon, gradually stir in enough of the remaining flour to make soft dough, mixing with hands if necessary.

● Turn out dough onto lightly floured surface; knead for 8 to 10 minutes or until smooth and elastic. Cover with tea towel; let rest for 10 minutes. Divide dough into 8 pieces; cut each into 9 to make 72 pieces.

● Using hands, press and pinch each into ball. Arrange three balls in cloverleaf pattern in each of 24 large greased muffin cups. Cover and let rise in warm draft-free place until doubled in bulk, 30 to 60 minutes.

● Brush with butter (if using). Bake in center of 400°F (200°C) oven for 10 to 12 minutes or until golden brown and rolls sound hollow when tapped on bottom. Remove from pan; let cool for 10 minutes on rack. Serve warm. *(Rolls can be individually wrapped in plastic wrap and frozen in rigid airtight container for up to 3 weeks.)* Makes 24 rolls.

BREAD MACHINE METHOD
(for dough only)

● Use 4-1/2 cups (1.125 L) all-purpose flour. Into pan of machine, add (in order) potatoes, milk, egg, shortening, sugar, salt, flour and yeast. (Do not let yeast touch liquid.) Choose dough setting. Remove from machine; shape and bake as directed.

A *touch of sweetness and an attractive cloverleaf shape make these rolls perfect for a holiday or celebration table.*

Per roll: about
- 144 calories
- 3 g protein
- 5 g fat
- 22 g carbohydrate

TIP: If you prefer larger rolls, cut the dough into only 54 pieces to make 18 rolls.

Classic Brioche à Tête

Imagine strolling by a Parisian bakery and spotting these glossy butter and egg-rich "buns," each sporting a jaunty topknot and fluted sides. Here's how to recreate that delicious moment at home.

Per bun: about
- 235 calories
- 12 g fat
- 6 g protein
- 27 g carbohydrate

1	pkg active dry yeast (or 1 tbsp/15 mL)	1
1/4 cup	granulated sugar	50 mL
2-1/2 tsp	salt	12 mL
5 cups	(approx) all-purpose flour	1.25 L
1 cup	hot water	250 mL
6	eggs	6
1 cup	butter, cut into pieces and softened	250 mL
2	egg yolks	2
1 tsp	water	5 mL

● In bowl of heavy-duty mixer and using paddle attachment, combine yeast, sugar, salt and 1 cup (250 mL) of the flour. Add hot water; beat at medium speed for 2 minutes or until smooth.

● Reduce speed to medium-low. Add eggs, one at a time, beating well after each addition. Gradually beat in 2 cups (500 mL) of the remaining flour. Add butter, a few pieces at a time, beating until completely incorporated. Gradually add remaining flour to make soft, very sticky dough. Cover with plastic wrap; let rise in warm draft-free place until doubled in bulk, about 3 hours.

● Gently deflate dough; cover and refrigerate for at least 6 hours or for up to 18 hours. *(Dough can be frozen for up to 2 weeks; thaw in refrigerator for 24 hours before proceeding.)*

● Turn out dough onto lightly floured surface. Using no more than 1/2 cup (125 mL) flour to keep hands floured during shaping, gently knead dough into ball. Divide into quarters. Roll each quarter into 12-inch (30 cm) long rope. Divide each rope into six 2-inch (5 cm) pieces; cut one of the pieces from each rope into 5 equal lengths. Shape all pieces into balls, making 20 large and 20 small.

● Place large balls in 20 well-greased brioche moulds or large muffin cups. Using scissors, cut X in top of each. Snuggle small ball into each X. Stir egg yolks with water; brush over brioche. Cover lightly and let rise in warm draft-free place until doubled in bulk, about 45 minutes.

● Bake in center of 400°F (200°C) oven for about 20 minutes or until golden. Let cool slightly in moulds on racks. Remove from moulds; let cool completely on racks. *(Brioche can be wrapped individually and frozen in rigid airtight container for up to 2 weeks.)* Makes 20 buns.

VARIATION

● BRANDIED APRICOT BRIOCHE À TÊTE: In saucepan, bring 2/3 cup (150 mL) finely diced dried apricots and 1/4 cup (50 mL) brandy just to boil. Reduce heat and simmer for about 1 minute or until brandy is absorbed. Let cool completely. Add to dough after turning out onto lightly floured surface; shape dough into rectangle and pour apricots onto center. Fold dough over apricots; knead until evenly distributed. Roll into ropes and proceed as in recipe, using no more than an extra 3/4 cup (175 mL) flour.

Chocolate Chelsea Christmas Tree ▼

1/4 cup	granulated sugar	50 mL
1 cup	warm milk	250 mL
1-1/2 tsp	active dry yeast	7 mL
1	egg	1
1/4 cup	butter, melted	50 mL
1 tsp	salt	5 mL
1 tsp	vanilla	5 mL
3 cups	(approx) all-purpose flour	750 mL
1/2 cup	unsweetened cocoa powder, sifted	125 mL
	FILLING	
1 cup	chocolate chips	250 mL
1/2 cup	packed brown sugar	125 mL
1/2 cup	dried cherries or raisins	125 mL
1/4 cup	chopped pecans	50 mL
1 tsp	cinnamon	5 mL
1/4 cup	butter, softened	50 mL
	TOPPING	
1/4 cup	corn syrup	50 mL
3/4 cup	icing sugar	175 mL
1 tbsp	milk	15 mL
8	candied cherries	8

● In large bowl, dissolve 1 tsp (5 mL) of the sugar in warm milk. Sprinkle in yeast; let stand for 10 minutes or until frothy. Whisk in egg, butter, remaining sugar, salt and vanilla. Gradually whisk in 1 cup (250 mL) of the flour. With wooden spoon, gradually beat in cocoa and enough of the remaining flour to make stiff dough.

● Turn out dough onto lightly floured surface; knead for about 5 minutes or until smooth and elastic. Place in greased bowl, turning to grease all over. Cover with plastic wrap; let rise in warm draft-free place until doubled in bulk, about 1 hour.

● FILLING: In bowl, mix together chocolate chips, sugar, cherries, pecans and cinnamon; set aside. Punch down dough; turn out onto lightly floured surface. Roll out into 14- x 12-inch (35 x 30 cm) rectangle. Spread

with butter, leaving 1-inch (2.5 cm) border uncovered; sprinkle filling over butter. Starting at long side, roll up tightly, pinching seam to seal. With serrated knife, cut into 16 slices.

● Center end slice near top (narrow end) of well-greased foil on large baking sheet. Reserve other end slice for "trunk." Arrange slices snugly in 4 more rows, adding 1 more slice for each row. Center reserved slice (trunk) lengthwise under tree. Cover lightly with plastic wrap; let rise for 20 minutes. Bake in center of 350°F (180°C) oven for 20 to 30 minutes or until firm to the touch.

● TOPPING: Slide buns and foil onto rack; brush with corn syrup. Let cool completely. Whisk icing sugar with milk. Using pastry bag, parchment-paper cone or spoon, pipe or drizzle icing decoratively over buns. Garnish with cherries. Make 16 buns.

BREAD MACHINE METHOD
(for dough only)

● Into pan of machine, add (in order) milk, egg, vanilla, butter, sugar, salt, flour, cocoa and 1-1/4 tsp (6 mL) quick-rising (active) dry yeast. (Do not let yeast touch liquid.) Choose dough setting, then turn out onto lightly floured surface and knead until smooth. Shape and bake as directed.

VARIATION

● CHOCOLATE CHELSEA BUNS: Follow recipe above but arrange slices, cut side down, in greased 9-inch (1.5 L) round cake pan.

W*ant to please a brunch crowd? Try mating the gooey appeal of a Chelsea bun with the irresistible attraction of chocolate. Shape into a tree for Christmas or arrange in a cake pan (see Variation, below) year round.*

Per bun: about
- 320 calories
- 12 g fat
- good source of iron
- 5 g protein
- 51 g carbohydrate

Cinnamon Buns ▼

There's something irresistible about cinnamon buns. Could it be the gooey caramelized coating, feathery light dough, crunchy pecans and generous amount of cinnamon? You bet!

Per bun: about
- 421 calories
- 6 g protein
- 22 g fat
- 52 g carbohydrate
- good source of iron

1/4 cup	granulated sugar	50 mL
1/2 cup	warm water	125 mL
1	pkg active dry yeast (or 1 tbsp/15 mL)	1
1/2 cup	milk	125 mL
1/4 cup	butter	50 mL
1 tsp	salt	5 mL
2	eggs, beaten	2
4 cups	(approx) all-purpose flour	1 L
	FILLING	
1 cup	butter	250 mL
1-1/2 cups	packed brown sugar	375 mL
1 cup	coarsely chopped pecans	250 mL
1 tbsp	cinnamon	15 mL

● In large bowl, dissolve 1 tsp (5 mL) of the sugar in warm water. Sprinkle in yeast; let stand for 10 minutes or until frothy. Meanwhile, in small saucepan, heat together milk, remaining sugar, butter and salt until butter is melted; let cool to lukewarm. Stir into yeast mixture along with eggs. With electric mixer, gradually beat in 1-1/2 cups (375 mL) of the flour; beat for 2 minutes or until smooth. With wooden spoon, gradually stir in enough of the remaining flour to make soft slightly sticky dough.

● Turn out dough onto lightly floured surface; knead for 7 to 10 minutes or until smooth and elastic. Place in large greased bowl, turning to grease all over. Cover lightly with plastic wrap; let rise in warm draft-free place until doubled in bulk, 1 to 1-1/2 hours (or in refrigerator for 8 hours or overnight).

● FILLING: Meanwhile, in saucepan over medium heat, melt 3/4 cup (175 mL) of the butter with 3/4 cup (175 mL) of the sugar, whisking until smooth. Pour into greased 13- x 9-inch (3 L) baking dish. Sprinkle with half of the pecans; set aside. Melt remaining butter; set aside. Combine remaining sugar, pecans and cinnamon; set aside.

● Punch down dough; turn out onto lightly floured surface. Roll out into 18- x 14-inch (45 x 35 cm) rectangle. Brush with all but 2 tbsp (25 mL) melted butter, leaving 1/2-inch (1 cm) border uncovered; sprinkle with sugar mixture. Starting at long side, tightly roll up, pinching seam to seal. Brush with remaining butter. With serrated knife, cut into 15 pieces; place, cut side down, in pan. Cover and let rise until doubled in bulk, about 1 hour.

● Bake in center of 375°F (190°C) oven for 25 to 30 minutes or until golden and top sounds hollow when tapped. Let stand in pan for 3 minutes. Invert onto serving platter, scraping off any remaining filling in pan to drizzle over buns. Makes 15 buns.

VARIATION
● CHELSEA BUNS: Omit pecans. Sprinkle 1 cup (250 mL) raisins or currants over sugar-coated dough before rolling up.

Hot Cross Buns ▼

1/2 cup	granulated sugar	125 mL
1/4 cup	warm water	50 mL
1	pkg active dry yeast (or 1 tbsp/15 mL)	1
3-1/2 cups	all-purpose flour	875 mL
2 tbsp	cinnamon	25 mL
1 tsp	nutmeg	5 mL
1/2 tsp	salt	2 mL
1/4 tsp	ground cloves	1 mL
3/4 cup	warm milk	175 mL
1/4 cup	butter, melted	50 mL
1	egg	1
1	egg yolk	1
1/2 cup	dried currants	125 mL
1/4 cup	chopped mixed candied peel	50 mL
	GLAZE	
2 tbsp	each granulated sugar and water	25 mL
	ICING	
1/2 cup	icing sugar	125 mL
2 tsp	water	10 mL

● In small bowl, dissolve 1 tbsp (15 mL) of the sugar in warm water. Sprinkle in yeast; let stand for 10 minutes or until frothy. Meanwhile, in large bowl, blend together remaining sugar, flour, cinnamon, nutmeg, salt and cloves; make well in center. Whisk together milk, butter, egg and egg yolk; pour into well. Pour in yeast mixture. With wooden spoon, stir until soft dough forms.

● Turn out dough onto lightly floured surface; knead for 8 minutes or until smooth and elastic. Place in greased bowl, turning to grease all over. Cover with plastic wrap; let rise in warm draft-free place until doubled in bulk, about 1 hour.

● Punch down dough; turn out onto lightly floured surface. Knead in currants and peel. Shape into 12-inch (30 cm) log; with serrated knife, cut into 9 pieces. Shape each into ball, stretching and pinching dough underneath to make tops smooth. Place 2 inches (5 cm)

apart on greased baking sheet. Cover and let rise until doubled in bulk, about 35 minutes. Bake in center of 400°F (200°C) oven for about 15 minutes or until golden brown.

● GLAZE: In saucepan, stir sugar with water over medium heat until dissolved; brush over buns. Let cool in pan.

● ICING: Stir icing sugar with water. Using piping bag fitted with round tip, pipe cross on top of each cooled bun. Makes 9 buns.

BREAD MACHINE METHOD FOR LOAF

● Reduce flour to 3-1/4 cups (800 mL). Into pan of machine, add (in order) water, milk, butter, sugar, eggs, salt, flour, cinnamon, nutmeg, cloves and yeast. (Do not let yeast touch liquid.) Choose sweet-dough setting; after first kneading, add currants and peel. Let baked loaf cool on rack. Makes 1 loaf.

O*ne a penny, two a penny, hot cross buns. Save a penny and make hot cross buns for everyone who loves the heavenly spice fragrance of this traditional currant-studded Easter treat.*

Per bun: about
- 353 calories
- 7 g fat
- good source of iron
- 7 g protein
- 65 g carbohydrate

TIP: To make 18 buns by hand, increase the yeast to 4 tsp (20 mL) and double the other ingredients.

Flatbreads

These are the most ancient of breads, and among the most delicious. Some flatbreads are more cracker than bread; others are slim loaves, tender, crusty and veiled with flour. Then there are puffy pitas, herb-sprinkled focaccia and much more to succeed with at home.

Wheat Tortillas ▶

While all kinds of flour tortillas now grace our grocery shelves, making your own is surprisingly easy.

Per tortilla: about
- 275 calories
- 6 g protein
- 9 g fat
- 42 g carbohydrate
- good source of iron

3-1/2 cups	all-purpose flour	875 mL
1-1/2 tsp	baking powder	7 mL
3/4 tsp	salt	4 mL
1/3 cup	shortening	75 mL
1-1/4 cups	water	300 mL

● In bowl, stir together flour, baking powder and salt; with pastry blender or two knives, cut in shortening until crumbly. Stir in water to make soft dough.

● Turn out dough onto lightly floured surface; knead just until dough comes together. Divide into 8 pieces; roll each into ball. Cover with tea towel; let rest for 30 minutes. Roll out each ball to 10-inch (25 cm) circle.

● Heat heavy skillet over medium heat. Peel tortilla from work surface by lifting closest edge away from you. Cook, one at a time, for 1 to 2 minutes per side or until speckled. Wrap in foil to keep soft, adding to stack as cooked. Makes 8 tortillas.

CHICKEN COUSCOUS WRAPS ▶
Soft wheat tortillas wrap around a zesty chicken-vegetable filling.

3	jalapeño peppers	3
1/4 cup	light mayonnaise	50 mL
1 tbsp	vegetable oil	15 mL
2 tsp	chili powder	10 mL
1/2 tsp	dried oregano	2 mL
3	boneless skinless chicken breasts	3
8	Wheat Tortillas	8
	FILLING	
2/3 cup	couscous	150 mL
1/4 tsp	salt	1 mL
2 tbsp	each vegetable oil and lime juice	25 mL
1/2 tsp	granulated sugar	2 mL

Pinch	pepper	Pinch
Half	avocado, diced	Half
1/2 cup	corn kernels	125 mL
1	plum tomato, diced	1

● Broil jalapeños, turning often, for 7 to 10 minutes or until blackened; let cool. Remove skins and seeds; chop finely. Stir 1 tsp (5 mL) into mayonnaise; set aside.

● FILLING: Mix couscous, salt and 2/3 cup (150 mL) boiling water, stirring once. Cover and set aside for 10 minutes. Whisk remaining jalapeño, oil, lime juice, 1 tbsp (15 mL) water, sugar and pepper; stir into couscous. Stir in avocado, corn and tomato.

● Meanwhile, mix oil, chili powder and oregano; brush onto chicken. Broil on greased baking sheet for 5 minutes per side or until no longer pink inside. Cut into strips.

● Spread mayonnaise mixture over tortillas, leaving 1-inch (2.5 cm) border. Starting just below center of each, mound filling in rectangle; top with chicken. Fold bottom border over filling, then sides; roll up. Makes 8 wraps.

Per wrap: about • 484 calories • 18 g protein • 19 g fat • 59 g carbohydrate • good source of iron

Easy Pita Bread ▼

Tiny enough to stuff for appetizers, generous enough to fill with lunchtime sandwich fixings, pita breads are always crowd-pleasing fare.

Per large pita: about
- 175 calories
- 4 g fat
- 4 g protein
- 30 g carbohydrate

1 tsp	granulated sugar	5 mL
2 cups	warm water	500 mL
1	pkg active dry yeast (or 1 tbsp/15 mL)	1
5 cups	(approx) all-purpose flour	1.25 L
1/4 cup	vegetable oil	50 mL
2 tsp	salt	10 mL

● In large bowl, dissolve sugar in warm water. Sprinkle in yeast; let stand for 10 minutes or until frothy. With electric mixer, beat in 2 cups (500 mL) of the flour, oil and salt; beat for about 3 minutes or until smooth. With wooden spoon, beat in enough of the remaining flour to make stiff dough.

● Turn out dough onto lightly floured surface; knead for about 10 minutes or until smooth and elastic. Place in greased bowl, turning to grease all over. Cover with plastic wrap; let rise in warm draft-free place until doubled in bulk, 1 to 1-1/2 hours.

● Punch down dough; turn out onto lightly floured surface. Divide into 16 or 32 pieces.

Roll out each piece into 7-inch (18 cm) or 4-inch (10 cm) round. Cover and let rise until slightly risen, about 15 minutes.

● Meanwhile, heat ungreased baking sheet on lowest rack in 500°F (260°C) oven. Using floured metal spatula, quickly transfer 2 or 3 pita rounds at a time to heated baking sheet; bake for 3 to 4 minutes or until puffed and light golden around edges. Let cool between damp tea towels. Pitas will collapse and soften slightly but pocket will remain. (If crisp pitas are desired, let cool on racks.) Makes sixteen 7-inch (18 cm) pitas or thirty-two 4-inch (10 cm) pitas.

VARIATIONS

● FIBER-RICH PITA BREAD: Substitute 1/2 cup (125 mL) natural bran, 1/2 cup (125 mL) rolled oats, 2 cups (500 mL) whole wheat flour and 2 cups (500 mL) all-purpose flour for 5 cups (1.25 L) all-purpose flour.

● MINI PITA BREAD: Once dough has risen in bowl, divide in half and roll each half into rectangle slightly less than 1/4 inch (5 mm) thick. Using floured 2-inch (5 cm) round cookie cutter, cut out rounds. Cover and let rise, then bake for 2 to 3 minutes. Makes about one hundred 2-inch (5 cm) mini pitas.

TIP: Serve tasty pita crisps hot as appetizers or store them in an airtight tin and serve with a dip for munching anytime. They're easy to make — just split baked pitas in half to make separate rounds. Brush with olive oil or melted butter; sprinkle with sesame seeds, poppy seeds or freshly grated Parmesan cheese. Cut each round into 4 or 8 wedges. Broil for 2 to 4 minutes or until light golden and crisp.

Chapati

1 cup	whole wheat flour	250 mL
Pinch	salt	Pinch
1/2 cup	(approx) water	125 mL

● Sift flour and salt onto work surface; make well in center. Pour in 1/2 cup (125 mL) water; using fingers, gradually draw flour into water until soft dough forms.

● On lightly floured surface, knead dough for about 15 minutes or until smooth and elastic. Gradually adding up to 2 tbsp (25 mL) water, knead for 10 minutes longer or until moist, pliable yet no longer sticky. Cover with plastic wrap; let rest for 30 minutes.

● Divide dough into 12 portions. On lightly floured surface, roll out each portion into 6-inch (15 cm) round. Heat ungreased skillet over medium-high heat; cook 1 round at a time for 30 to 40 seconds or until bubbles appear on surface. Using spatula, flatten bubbles; turn over and cook for 30 to 40 seconds or until second side is lightly browned. *(Chapati can be cooled and stored in plastic bag for up to 8 hours. To reheat, place on baking sheet; cover loosely with foil and bake in 350°F/180°C oven for 5 to 10 minutes or until heated through.)* Makes 12 chapati.

T*his simple unleavened whole wheat bread is "baked" on a hot griddle in India, but a dry skillet works just as well. Serve warm with melted butter.*

Per chapati: about
- 34 calories
- 1 g protein
- trace fat
- 7 g carbohydrate

Naan Bread

2 tbsp	granulated sugar	25 mL
1-1/2 cups	warm water	375 mL
1 tbsp	active or quick-rising (instant) dry yeast	15 mL
1	egg yolk	1
2 tbsp	butter, melted	25 mL
2-1/2 tsp	salt	12 mL
3/4 cup	warm whipping cream	175 mL
1/4 cup	warm milk	50 mL
6 cups	(approx) all-purpose flour	1.5 L
2-1/2 tsp	baking powder	12 mL

● In large bowl, dissolve 1 tsp (5 mL) of the sugar in warm water. Sprinkle in yeast; let stand for 10 minutes or until frothy. Whisk in remaining sugar, egg yolk, butter and salt. Stir in warm cream and milk. With wooden spoon, stir in 5 cups (1.25 L) of the flour and baking powder to make soft dough.

● Turn out dough onto lightly floured surface; knead for 10 to 12 minutes or until smooth and elastic, adding enough of the remaining flour as necessary. Place in greased bowl, turning to grease all over.

Cover with plastic wrap; let rise in warm draft-free place until doubled in bulk, about 45 minutes. *(Alternatively, place unrisen dough in greased plastic bag and refrigerate for up to 1 day; let come to room temperature to proceed.)*

● Punch down dough; turn out onto lightly floured surface. Knead into ball. Divide dough into 8 pieces; roll into balls. Cover and let rest for 10 minutes. Gently stretch or roll into teardrop shape about 1/4 inch (5 mm) thick. Place on foil- or parchment paper-lined baking sheets; cover and let rest for 15 minutes. Bake on lowest rack in 400°F (200°C) oven for about 10 minutes or until puffed and golden. Makes 8 servings.

VARIATION

● GRILLED NAAN BREAD: To grill on the barbecue, place dough directly on greased grill over medium-high heat; close lid and bake for 3 to 4 minutes per side or until puffed and no longer moist and doughy inside.

M*y, how breads travel. From India comes this teardrop-shaped naan bread, where it is served hot off the sides of a tandoor oven. Many communities in Canada now have restaurants with tandoor ovens, so an authentic sampling of this bread is possible. Serve it with curries or any grilled meat, chicken or fish.*

Per serving: about
- 470 calories
- 11 g protein
- 13 g fat
- 77 g carbohydrate
- excellent source of iron

Middle Eastern Flatbread ▶

Puffed like duvets, these flatbreads are delicious on their own, in the style of the Middle East with a smear of hummus or thick yogurt, or simply topped with fresh tomatoes, salt, pepper and olive oil.

Per serving: about
- 435 calories
- 9 g protein
- 13 g fat
- 68 g carbohydrate
- excellent source of iron

2 tsp	granulated sugar	10 mL
2 cups	warm water	500 mL
1 tbsp	active or quick-rising (instant) dry yeast	15 mL
2 tbsp	olive oil	25 mL
2 tsp	salt	10 mL
5-1/2 cups	(approx) all-purpose flour	1.375 L
	TOPPING	
1/3 cup	extra virgin olive oil	75 mL
3 tbsp	lemon juice	50 mL
2 tbsp	zahtar spice	25 mL
1/4 tsp	salt	1 mL

● In large bowl, dissolve sugar in warm water. Sprinkle in yeast; let stand for 10 minutes or until frothy. Whisk in oil and salt. With wooden spoon, stir in 4-1/2 cups (1.125 L) of the flour to make soft dough.

● Turn out dough onto lightly floured surface; knead for 8 to 10 minutes or until smooth and elastic, adding enough of the remaining flour as necessary. Place in lightly greased bowl, turning to grease all over. Cover with plastic wrap; let rise in warm draft-free place until doubled in bulk, about 45 minutes. *(Alternatively, place unrisen dough in greased plastic bag and refrigerate for up to 1 day; let come to room temperature to proceed.)*

● Punch down dough; turn out onto lightly floured surface. Knead into ball; flatten into rough circle. With serrated knife, cut into 8 wedges; gently stretch or roll out each into 1/4-inch (5 mm) thick irregular triangle. Place on foil- or parchment paper-lined baking sheets; cover and let rest for 15 minutes.

● TOPPING: Stir together oil, lemon juice, zahtar spice and salt; brush over triangles. Bake on lowest rack in 425°F (220°C) oven for 10 minutes or until golden. Makes 8 servings.

VARIATION

● GRILLED MIDDLE EASTERN FLATBREAD: To grill on the barbecue, place dough directly on greased grill over medium-high heat; close lid and cook for 1 to 2 minutes per side or until beginning to brown, brushing with more topping if desired.

TIP: You can find zahtar spice at a Middle Eastern market or through mail-order sources — or substitute other herb mixes such as herbes de Provence or Italian herbs for a different but equally delicious flatbread.

Round Moroccan Loaves

In Morocco, it's a familiar site to see children hurrying along the road, balancing a board covered with a clean towel. Underneath are discs of bread dough, kneaded, shaped and proofed at home, on their way to the neighborhood bakery. Traditionally served with tagine (a deliciously spicy stew), Moroccan bread can be served with any dish that begs to be mopped up and enjoyed.

Per slice: about
- 116 calories
- 3 g fat
- 3 g protein
- 20 g carbohydrate

1 tsp	granulated sugar	5 mL
2 cups	warm water	500 mL
1	pkg active dry yeast	1
1 cup	whole wheat flour	250 mL
1/4 cup	olive oil	50 mL
1 tbsp	aniseed	15 mL
2 tsp	salt	10 mL
1 tsp	sesame seeds	5 mL
4 cups	(approx) unbleached all-purpose flour	1 L
	Cornmeal	

● In large bowl, dissolve sugar in warm water. Sprinkle in yeast; let stand for 10 minutes or until frothy. With electric mixer, beat in whole wheat flour, oil, aniseed, salt and sesame seeds. Beat in 2 cups (500 mL) of the all-purpose flour, 1/2 cup (125 mL) at a time. With wooden spoon, gradually stir in enough of the remaining flour to make stiff dough.

● Turn out dough onto lightly floured surface; knead for 10 minutes or until smooth and elastic. Place in greased bowl, turning to grease all over. Cover with plastic wrap; let rise in warm draft-free place until doubled in bulk, about 1-1/2 hours.

● Punch down dough; turn out onto floured surface. Knead into ball; divide in half. Form each into ball; let rest for 5 to 10 minutes if dough is too elastic to roll. Roll out each half into rounds about 3/4 inch (2 cm) thick. Place each on cornmeal-dusted baking sheet. Cover and let rise in warm draft-free place until doubled in bulk, 45 to 60 minutes.

● Prick rounds with fork in 4 spots around edge; bake in center of 400°F (200°C) oven for 10 minutes. Reduce heat to 325°F (160°C); bake for about 25 minutes or until golden and loaves sound hollow when tapped on bottom. Remove from pan; let cool on racks. Makes 2 loaves, 12 slices each.

Persian Flatbread

Long flatbreads that are easy to cut crosswise into two-finger-size strips go as well with dinner as they do with dips, soups and chili.

Per serving: about
- 239 calories
- 2 g fat
- good source of iron
- 8 g protein
- 49 g carbohydrate
- high source of fiber

Pinch	granulated sugar	Pinch
2-1/2 cups	warm water	625 mL
1-1/2 tsp	active dry yeast	7 mL
4-1/4 cups	all-purpose flour`	1.05 L
2 cups	whole wheat flour	500 mL
1 tbsp	salt	15 mL
2 tbsp	sesame seeds	25 mL

● In large bowl, dissolve sugar in 1/4 cup (50 mL) of the water. Sprinkle in yeast; let stand for 10 minutes or until frothy. Stir in remaining water. With wooden spoon, stir in all-purpose flour, whole wheat flour and salt to form shaggy wet dough.

● Turn out dough onto floured surface. Knead for 5 minutes or until smooth, soft, moist and sticky. Form into ball. Place in greased bowl, turning to grease all over. Cover with plastic wrap; let rise in warm draft-free place until doubled in bulk, about 1 hour.

● Punch down dough; turn out onto lightly floured surface. Divide in half; shape each into 8-inch (20 cm) long oval. Gently stretch each into 16- x 7-inch (40 x 18 cm) oval about 1/2 inch (1 cm) thick. Place each on lightly greased rimless baking sheet (or inverted rimmed baking sheet), reshaping if necessary. Brush with water; sprinkle evenly with sesame seeds. Let rise for 10 minutes.

● With fingertips, make deep indentations all over dough to give dimpled effect. Bake, one sheet at a time, in center of 450°F (230°C) oven for about 10 minutes or until crust is set but still pale. Slip off baking sheet directly onto rack. Bake for about 6 minutes longer or until bottom is golden brown and crisp and top is golden in spots. Makes 2 flatbreads, 6 servings each.

Crisp Seeded Cracker Bread

3-3/4 cups	(approx) all-purpose flour	925 mL
1 tsp	salt	5 mL
1-1/2 cups	water	375 mL
1	egg white, beaten	1
1/2 cup	sesame or poppy seeds (optional)	125 mL

● In food processor, pulse 3-1/2 cups (875 mL) of the flour and salt to combine. With motor running, add water in steady stream until dough forms into ball. Pulse in enough of the remaining flour, 1 tbsp (15 mL) at a time, until dough is no longer sticky. Process for 1 minute.

● Turn out dough onto lightly floured surface; knead into ball. Cover with plastic wrap; let rest for 30 minutes.

● Divide dough into 6 pieces. Leaving remaining pieces covered with plastic wrap, roll out 1 piece to 14- x 9-inch (35 x 23 cm) rectangle; place on greased baking sheet. Brush lightly with some of the egg white; sprinkle with some of the sesame seeds (if using). Bake in center of 500°F (260°C) oven for about 6 minutes or until browned at edges and golden brown blisters appear all over. Let cool on pan on rack.

● Repeat with remaining dough. Break into long shards. *(Crackers can be stored in airtight container for up to 2 weeks.)* Makes about 48 pieces.

When cookbook author and flatbread expert Jeffrey Alford made food processor crackers on Canadian Living TV, we were inspired to create this easy non-yeasted bread.

Per piece: about
- 30 calories
- trace fat
- 1 g protein
- 6 g carbohydrate

Caramelized Onion Focaccia

2 tbsp	olive oil	25 mL
3	large onions, thinly sliced	3
1 tbsp	soy sauce	15 mL
1-1/2 tsp	dried sage	7 mL
1 tsp	cider vinegar	5 mL
1/4 tsp	(approx) salt	1 mL
Pinch	pepper	Pinch
1 tbsp	chopped fresh parsley	15 mL
1/3 cup	whole wheat flour	75 mL
1/3 cup	warm water	75 mL
2 tsp	active dry yeast	10 mL
1/4 cup	warm milk	50 mL
1-1/2 cups	all-purpose flour	375 mL

● In large nonstick skillet, heat half of the oil over medium heat; cook onions, stirring occasionally, for 5 minutes. Stir in soy sauce, sage, vinegar, pinch of the salt and the pepper. Cover and cook over low heat, stirring, for about 25 minutes or until very soft, adding 1 tbsp (15 mL) water if needed to prevent sticking. Stir in parsley.

● In large bowl, stir together whole wheat flour, water and yeast; cover and let rest for 30 minutes. Stir in milk, remaining oil, 1/4 tsp (1 mL) salt and 1 cup (250 mL) of the all-purpose flour, mixing well.

● Turn out dough onto lightly floured surface; knead for 7 to 10 minutes or until soft and slightly sticky, adding enough of the remaining flour as necessary. Place in greased bowl, turning to grease all over. Cover with plastic wrap; let rise in warm draft-free place until doubled in bulk, about 1 hour.

● Punch down dough; turn out onto lightly floured surface. Roll out into rectangle about 1/4 inch (5 mm) thick. Transfer to floured baking sheet; cover and let rise until doubled in bulk, about 30 minutes. Press fingertips into dough to create dimples. Bake in 400°F (200°C) oven for 15 to 20 minutes or until golden brown. Remove from pan; let cool on rack. Spread with onion mixture. Cut into fingers. Makes 40 pieces.

Slow frying in very little oil brings out the sweetness in onions — an inexpensive and grand topping. A garnish of sliced olives is nice, too.

Per piece: about
- 30 calories
- 1 g fat
- 1 g protein
- 6 g carbohydrate

Busy-Day Focaccia

*H*ey, cheat a little with
ready-made pizza dough,
available refrigerated or
frozen at your local
supermarket.

Per piece: about
• 146 calories   • 4 g protein
• 3 g fat   • 26 g carbohydrate

1 lb	pizza dough	500 g
2 tsp	(approx) olive oil	10 mL
1/4 tsp	coarse salt (optional)	1 mL
1/2 cup	thinly sliced red onion	125 mL
1/4 cup	coarsely chopped black olives	50 mL
1 tsp	minced fresh rosemary (or 1/4 tsp/1 mL dried)	5 mL

● Pat dough evenly into lightly greased 9-inch (2.5 L) square cake pan. Cover with plastic wrap; let rise for 30 minutes.

● With fingertip, make 12 indents in dough. Brush with oil. Sprinkle with salt (if using), red onion, olives and rosemary. Bake in 450°F (230°C) oven for 30 to 40 minutes or until golden brown. Remove from pan; let cool slightly on rack. Cut into 4 strips; cut each in half. Serve warm. Makes 8 pieces.

Fabulous Focaccia ◀

1 tsp	granulated sugar	5 mL
1 cup	warm water	250 mL
1	pkg active dry yeast (or 1 tbsp/15 mL)	1
2-1/2 cups	all-purpose flour	625 mL
2 tbsp	olive oil	25 mL
1 tsp	salt	5 mL
1/2 tsp	each dried sage, rosemary and marjoram	2 mL
2 tbsp	cornmeal	25 mL
	TOPPING	
3 tbsp	olive oil	50 mL
1	onion, thinly sliced	1
1/2 tsp	dried rosemary	2 mL

● In large bowl, dissolve sugar in warm water. Sprinkle in yeast; let stand for 10 minutes or until frothy. With electric mixer, beat in 1 cup (250 mL) of the flour; beat for 2 minutes or until smooth. Cover with plastic wrap; let rise in warm draft-free place until doubled in bulk, about 30 minutes. With wooden spoon, stir in oil, salt, sage, rosemary, marjoram and 1 cup (250 mL) of the flour.

● Turn out dough onto lightly floured surface; knead for 5 minutes or until smooth and soft, adding enough of the remaining flour as necessary. Place in greased bowl, turning to grease all over. Cover with plastic wrap; let rise in warm draft-free place until doubled in bulk, about 1 hour.

● Gently punch down dough; turn out onto lightly floured surface. Divide in half; cover with tea towel and let rest for 5 minutes. Roll out each half into rough 8-inch (20 cm) circle 1/2 inch (1 cm) thick, or roll each half into 3 smaller circles. Sprinkle cornmeal over baking sheet; place rounds on top. Cover and let rise until doubled in bulk, about 30 minutes.

● TOPPING: Meanwhile, in small skillet, heat oil over medium-low heat; cook onion and rosemary, stirring occasionally, for 7 to 10 minutes or until softened and golden. Let cool.

● Press fingertips into dough almost to bottom to give dimpled effect. Top with onion mixture. Bake on lowest rack in 400°F (200°C) oven for about 20 minutes or until golden and focaccias sound hollow when tapped on bottom. Makes 6 servings.

VARIATIONS

● SWEET PEPPER AND THYME FOCACCIA: Brush dough with 1 tbsp (15 mL) olive oil. Scatter 1 small thinly sliced sweet red pepper over top. Sprinkle with fresh thyme sprigs (or 1/2 tsp/2 mL dried thyme). Bake as directed.

● SEA SALT FOCACCIA: Brush dough with 1 tbsp (15 mL) olive oil; sprinkle with 1/4 tsp (1 mL) coarse sea salt, and pinch of coarsely ground pepper if desired. Bake as directed.

Cooking cousin of the pizza, focaccia is Italian flatbread with flair. The rounds are crusty on the bottom, dimpled on the top and lightly sprinkled with olive oil, herbs such as sage and rosemary, or simply coarse salt.

Per serving: about
- 314 calories
- 6 g protein
- 12 g fat
- 45 g carbohydrate
- good source of iron

TIPS
● Unlike pizza, which is a meal in itself, focaccia is a bread to go with dinner, or to split in half for a sunny Mediterranean sandwich filled with grilled vegetables, salami or ham, tomatoes and arugula. Or, cut into appetizer-size wedges and enjoy with a glass of wine, and perhaps a sliver of Asiago cheese.
● Making a spongy dough mixture, or sponge, before adding all the flour and flavorings allows the yeast to develop and gives the bread a better texture. Letting dough rest for 5 minutes before rolling out makes it easier to shape.
● Cornmeal on the baking sheet prevents the bread from sticking and adds texture to the crust.
● Baking the bread on the lowest rack makes it crusty.

Ciabatta

Let us introduce you to the new darling of the flatbread family — ciabatta, or Italian slipper bread. An excellent dinner bread, or sliced through for sandwiches, it features a crusty floured surface and holey crumb.

Per serving: about
• 205 calories   • 6 g protein
• 2 g fat   • 39 g carbohydrate

SPONGE		
1/4 tsp	active dry yeast	1 mL
2/3 cup	warm water	150 mL
1-1/4 cups	all-purpose flour	300 mL

DOUGH		
Pinch	granulated sugar	Pinch
1/2 cup	warm water	125 mL
1/2 tsp	active dry yeast	2 mL
1/4 cup	milk	50 mL
1 tbsp	olive oil	15 mL
2 cups	all-purpose flour	500 mL
1-1/2 tsp	salt	7 mL

● SPONGE: In bowl, stir yeast into warm water until dissolved; stir in flour until smooth. Cover with plastic wrap and refrigerate for at least 12 hours or for up to 24 hours.

● DOUGH: In bowl of electric mixer, dissolve sugar in warm water. Sprinkle in yeast; let stand for 10 minutes or until frothy. Using dough hook on low speed, stir in sponge, milk and oil until combined. Add flour and salt; mix on low speed for 8 minutes, scraping down bowl halfway through.

● Turn out dough onto well-floured surface; knead lightly into ball. Place in greased bowl, turning to grease all over. Cover with plastic wrap; let rise in warm draft-free place until doubled in bulk and bubbles appear on surface, about 1-1/2 hours.

● Scrape dough out of bowl onto lightly floured surface; divide in half. With floured hands, gently form each into cylinder, pinching seam to seal. Pull each out to 9- x 4-inch (23 x 10 cm) rectangle. Place each, seam side up, on well-floured tea towel. Cover with damp tea towel; let rise until not quite doubled in bulk and bubbles appear on surface, about 1-1/2 hours.

● Flip rectangles gently over onto two floured baking sheets. Spray with water. Bake on bottom third and middle racks of 425°F (220°C) oven for 10 minutes. Switch position of sheets; spray with water. Bake for 12 to 15 minutes longer or until golden brown and bread sounds hollow when tapped on bottom. Let cool on racks. Makes 2 loaves, 4 servings each.

VARIATION

● CIABATTA BUNS: Similar to flat Portuguese pada buns, these buns of two attached balls of dough make delicious sandwiches. They can also be pulled into two smaller buns to use as dinner rolls or for smaller appetites.

● Make dough through to first rise. Scrape onto well-floured surface; divide into 8 pieces. Pull edges of one piece over center, pinching to seal and forming small ball. Holding sealed portion, dip smooth underside into about 1/4 cup (50 mL) all-purpose flour to coat. Place on greased baking sheet, floured side up.

● Repeat with second ball, placing on sheet to just touch first ball. Repeat with dough to form 4 buns of 2 attached pieces each.

● Cover with tea towel; let rise in warm draft-free place until not quite doubled in bulk and bubbles are visible just below surface, about 1 hour. Bake for 25 minutes or until golden and buns sound hollow when tapped on bottom. Makes 4 buns.

Provençale Olive Fougasse ▼

1/4 tsp	granulated sugar	1 mL
1-1/4 cups	warm water	300 mL
2-1/2 tsp	active dry yeast	12 mL
3 tbsp	olive oil	50 mL
3-1/4 cups	all-purpose flour	800 mL
3/4 tsp	salt	4 mL
1/2 cup	chopped pitted black olives	125 mL
2 tbsp	milk	25 mL

● In large bowl, dissolve sugar in warm water. Sprinkle in yeast; let stand for 10 minutes or until frothy. Stir in oil. Stir in 3 cups (750 mL) of the flour and salt to form moist dough.

● Turn out dough onto lightly floured surface. Knead for about 8 minutes or until smooth and elastic yet still slightly moist, dusting with as much of the remaining flour as necessary to prevent sticking. Cover with tea towel; let rest for 5 minutes.

● Flatten dough into disk; sprinkle with olives. Fold dough over; knead for 3 minutes or until olives are evenly distributed. Form into ball. Place in greased bowl, turning to grease all over. Cover with plastic wrap; let rise in warm draft-free place until doubled in bulk, about 45 minutes.

● Punch down dough; turn out onto lightly floured surface. Stretch into 12- x 8-inch (30 x 20 cm) rectangle. Leaving 1-inch (2.5 cm) border all around, cut center of rectangle completely through to work surface into 2 rows of 4 diagonal slashes each. Cut 1-inch (2.5 cm) notches into edge of dough between slashes.

Gently lift onto greased 17- x 11-inch (45 x 29 cm) baking sheet. Pull slashes open by at least 1 inch (2.5 cm). Cover and let rise in warm draft-free place for 20 minutes.

● Brush with milk. Bake in center of 450°F (230°C) oven for about 20 minutes or until golden and bread sounds hollow when tapped on bottom. Makes 1 loaf, 10 servings.

B*akeries in the south of France specialize in this satisfyingly chewy ladder-shaped bread. It features two regional products — olive oil and olives. Enjoy it as an appetizer with a glass of wine, or serve to acclaim for any special outdoor or indoor occasion.*

Per serving:
about
- 195 calories
- 5 g protein
- 5 g fat
- 32 g carbohydrate

Pizzas and Friends

From a simple glaze of tomatoes and a sprinkle of cheese to mushrooms galore, thick juicy sausages, smoky grilled vegetables, pesto and pepperoni and cheeses — these pizzas are always people-pleasing and easy to make.

*F*rank Colonardi, manager of Serra, a delightful Toronto restaurant specializing in wood-burning-oven pizzas, created this highly original and absolutely delicious pizza. Topping flavors are pure Southeast Asian with Italian mozzarella and a crunchy crust tying it together into one satisfying package.

Per slice: about
- 218 calories
- 8 g fat
- 15 g protein
- 21 g carbohydrate

Spicy Peanut Chicken Pizza

2	boneless skinless chicken breasts	2
Pinch	each salt and pepper	Pinch
3 tbsp	prepared spicy peanut sauce	50 mL
1	unbaked 12-inch (30 cm) pizza base (see Pizza Doughs, p. 73)	1
1-1/2 cups	shredded mozzarella cheese	375 mL
1/2 cup	shredded carrot	125 mL
2	green onions, thinly sliced	2
1/2 cup	bean sprouts	125 mL
2 tbsp	chopped fresh coriander or parsley	25 mL

● Sprinkle chicken with salt and pepper. Place on lightly greased grill over medium-high heat (or on baking sheet under broiler); close lid and cook for about 4 minutes per side or until no longer pink inside. Let cool slightly. Cut crosswise into 1/4-inch (5 mm) thick strips.

● Spread peanut sauce evenly over pizza base. Sprinkle with 1 cup (250 mL) of the mozzarella, then chicken, carrot, onions, then remaining mozzarella. Bake in bottom third of 500°F (260°C) oven for about 10 minutes or until cheese is bubbly and crust is golden and slightly puffed. Sprinkle with bean sprouts and coriander. Makes 8 slices.

(Clockwise from top right) Spicy Peanut Chicken Pizza; Pesto and Roasted Eggplant Pizza (p. 81); Greek Pizza (p. 72); and Hot Italian Sausage Pizza (p. 72)

Greek Pizza

*O*regano, tomatoes, black olives and feta cheese shift pizza's appeal to Greece.

Per slice: about
- 272 calories
- 15 g fat
- good source of calcium
- 11 g protein
- 22 g carbohydrate

Half	sweet green pepper	Half
2 tbsp	olive oil	25 mL
1 tsp	dried oregano	5 mL
1	unbaked 12-inch (30 cm) pizza base (see Pizza Doughs, p. 73)	1
2 cups	shredded mozzarella cheese	500 mL
3	tomatoes, thinly sliced	3
1/3 cup	black olives, pitted and sliced	75 mL
1 cup	crumbled feta cheese	250 mL

● Cut green pepper in half lengthwise; thinly slice crosswise. Set aside.

● Stir together oil and oregano; brush over pizza base. Sprinkle with mozzarella cheese. Arrange tomatoes in overlapping concentric circles over mozzarella. Sprinkle with olives and green pepper; sprinkle with feta cheese.

● Bake in bottom third of 500°F (260°C) oven for 10 minutes or until feta is soft and crust is golden and slightly puffed. Makes 8 slices.

Hot Italian Sausage Pizza ▼

*R*obust and so satisfying, this sausage (your choice of spiciness), sweet pepper, red onion and mozzarella-topped Serra pizza is one of the restaurant's most popular.

Per slice: about
- 355 calories
- 21 g fat
- good source of calcium
- 14 g protein
- 28 g carbohydrate

1	each sweet red and green pepper	1
1	red onion	1
2 tbsp	olive oil	25 mL
1	small clove garlic, minced	1
1 tsp	minced jalapeño pepper (or 1/4 tsp/1 mL hot pepper sauce)	5 mL
8 oz	hot or mild Italian sausage	250 g
1	unbaked 12-inch (30 cm) pizza base (see Pizza Doughs, p. 73)	1
1/2 cup	pizza or pasta sauce	125 mL
2 cups	shredded mozzarella cheese	500 mL
2 tbsp	chopped fresh parsley	25 mL

● Core and cut red and green peppers into quarters. Cut onion into 1/2-inch (1 cm) thick slices. Whisk together oil, garlic and jalapeño pepper; brush over vegetables.

● Place peppers on greased grill over medium-high heat; close lid and cook for 5 minutes. Add onion and sausage; cook, covered and turning occasionally, for about 15 minutes or until vegetables are tender and sausage is no longer pink inside. Let cool.

● Cut peppers into thin slices. Separate onion into rings. Cut sausage on diagonal into 1/4-inch (5 mm) thick slices. Spread pizza base with sauce; sprinkle with onion, then mozzarella cheese, sweet peppers and sausage.

● Bake in bottom third of 500°F (260°C) oven for 10 minutes or until cheese is bubbly and crust is golden and slightly puffed. Sprinkle with parsley. Makes 8 slices.

PIZZA DOUGHS

Choose the dough that suits the amount of time you have, your kitchen equipment and your pleasure.
Each of the recipes below makes a fairly thin (rather than thick) puffy pizza base.

BREAD MACHINE DOUGH

1 cup	water	250 mL
1 tbsp	olive oil	15 mL
1 tsp	salt	5 mL
3 cups	all-purpose flour	750 mL
2 tsp	quick-rising (instant) dry yeast	10 mL
2 tsp	cornmeal	10 mL

● Into pan of machine, add (in order) water, oil, salt, flour and yeast. (Do not let yeast touch liquid.) Choose dough setting.

● Turn out dough onto lightly floured surface; divide in half and shape each into disc. Roll out each disc into 12-inch (30 cm) circle, letting dough rest, covered, if too elastic to roll.

● Sprinkle two 12-inch (30 cm) pizza pans with cornmeal; center dough on each. Let rest for 15 minutes. Press all over to form slightly raised rim. Makes 1-1/2 lb (750 g) dough, enough for two 12-inch (30 cm) thin pizza bases or one slightly thicker 15- x 10-inch (38 x 25 cm) base.

FOOD PROCESSOR DOUGH

1/2 cup	water	125 mL
1-1/2 tsp	olive oil	7 mL
1-1/2 cups	all-purpose flour	375 mL
1 tsp	quick-rising (instant) dry yeast	5 mL
1/2 tsp	salt	2 mL

● In small saucepan, heat water with oil until at 120°F (50°C). In food processor, pulse together flour, yeast and salt just until blended. With motor running, pour in water mixture; whirl for 1 minute or until ball forms.

● With floured hands, shape into smooth ball. Place in greased bowl, turning to grease all over. Cover with plastic wrap; let rise in warm draft-free place until doubled in bulk, about 1 hour. Roll out as for Bread Machine Dough. Makes 12 oz (375 g) dough, enough for one 12-inch (30 cm) thin pizza base. Repeat recipe for two pizza bases.

HANDMADE DOUGH

1/2 cup	water	125 mL
1-1/2 tsp	olive oil	7 mL
1-1/2 cups	all-purpose flour	375 mL
1 tsp	quick-rising (instant) dry yeast	5 mL
1/2 tsp	salt	2 mL

● In small saucepan, heat water with oil until at 120°F (50°C). In large bowl, combine flour, yeast and salt. With wooden spoon, gradually stir in water mixture until dough forms (you may need to use hands).

● Turn out dough onto lightly floured surface; knead for about 8 minutes or until smooth and elastic. Place in greased bowl, turning to grease all over. Cover with plastic wrap; let rise in warm draft-free place until doubled in bulk, about 1 hour. Roll out as for Bread Machine Dough. Makes 12 oz (375 g) dough, enough for one 12-inch (30 cm) thin pizza base. Double ingredients for two pizza bases.

Woodland Mushroom Pizza

1 lb	fresh exotic mushrooms	500 g
1 tbsp	olive oil	15 mL
3	cloves garlic, minced	3
3 cups	sliced button mushrooms	750 mL
1	unbaked 12-inch (30 cm) pizza base (see Pizza Doughs, above)	1
1/2 cup	pizza or pasta sauce	125 mL
1 cup	shredded mozzarella cheese	250 mL
2 oz	feta cheese (or 1/4 cup/50 mL freshly grated Parmesan cheese)	60 g
2 tbsp	chopped fresh thyme, basil or oregano	25 mL

● Brush mushrooms clean. Discard stems if tough; slice caps. In large skillet, heat oil over medium-high heat; cook garlic, exotic and button mushrooms for about 15 minutes or until tender and liquid is evaporated.

● Spread pizza base with sauce; sprinkle with mushrooms, then mozzarella cheese. Crumble feta cheese over top.

● Bake in bottom third of 500°F (260°C) oven for 10 minutes or until crust is golden and slightly puffed and cheese is bubbly. Sprinkle with thyme. Makes 8 slices.

Cultivated exotic mushrooms — shiitake, oyster, cremini and portobello — add a delicious woodsiness to this signature pizza from Toronto's Serra restaurant.

Per slice: about
- 205 calories
- 8 g protein
- 9 g fat
- 25 g carbohydrate
- good source of iron

Tapenade and Grilled Vegetable Pizza

*T*apenade (black olive paste), like pesto, is a high-octane flavor — and in this pizza from Toronto's Serra restaurant, you can interchange them. In the cold months when the barbecue is indoors, roast the vegetables or replace with artichoke hearts.

Per slice: about
- 235 calories
- 7 g protein
- 12 g fat
- 27 g carbohydrate
- good source of iron
- high source of fiber

1	large zucchini	1
Half	small eggplant	Half
1	sweet green or red pepper	1
1	large portobello mushroom	1
1/4 cup	olive oil	50 mL
2	cloves garlic, minced	2
1/4 tsp	each salt and pepper	1 mL
3	canned artichokes, quartered	3
2	plum tomatoes, diced	2
3 tbsp	tapenade (prepared black olive paste)	50 mL
1	unbaked 12-inch (30 cm) pizza base (see Pizza Doughs, p. 73)	1
4 oz	feta cheese, crumbled	125 g
2 tbsp	shredded fresh basil	25 mL

● Cut zucchini into 1/4-inch (5 mm) thick slices. Cut eggplant into 1/2-inch (1 cm) thick slices. Core and quarter green pepper. Brush portobello mushroom clean; discard stem. Combine oil and garlic; brush over vegetables. Sprinkle with salt and pepper.

● Place green pepper on greased grill over medium-low heat; close lid and cook for 8 minutes. Add eggplant; cook for 4 minutes. Add mushroom; cook for 2 minutes. Add zucchini; cook for 6 minutes or until all vegetables are tender, turning occasionally.

● Slice mushroom, green pepper and eggplant into 1/2-inch (1 cm) thick strips; place in bowl. Add zucchini, artichokes and tomatoes; toss to combine.

● Spread tapenade over pizza base; mound vegetable mixture on top. Sprinkle with feta cheese.

● Bake in bottom third of 500°F (260°C) oven for 10 minutes or until crust is golden and slightly puffed and cheese is melted. Sprinkle with basil. Makes 8 slices.

VARIATION
● TAPENADE AND ARTICHOKE PIZZA: Replace grilled vegetables with 1 can (19 oz/540 mL) artichoke hearts, well-drained and quartered.

Tex-Mex Corn Pizza

*W*hether you use fresh, frozen or canned corn, you can enjoy a south-of-the-border vegetable-rich pizza any time of the year.

Per serving: about
- 380 calories
- 19 g protein
- 10 g fat
- 56 g carbohydrate
- high source of fiber
- excellent source of calcium
- good source of iron

1	12-inch (30 cm) prebaked pizza base	1
4 tsp	Dijon mustard	20 mL
1-1/4 cups	shredded light Monterey Jack-style cheese	300 mL
2 cups	cooked corn kernels	500 mL
3	green onions, chopped	3
1/4 cup	chopped fresh coriander or parsley	50 mL
2 tbsp	chopped canned green chilies or pickled jalapeño peppers	25 mL
1	large tomato, sliced	1
1	sweet green pepper, cut in rings	1

● Place pizza base on pizza pan or baking sheet. Brush with mustard; sprinkle with 1/2 cup (125 mL) of the cheese.

● In bowl, toss together corn, onions, coriander and chilies. Arrange tomato slices in single layer over base, overlapping slightly; repeat with green pepper. Spoon corn mixture evenly over top. Sprinkle with remaining cheese.

● Bake in bottom third of 425°F (220°C) oven for 12 to 15 minutes or until crust is crisp and cheese is melted. Makes 4 servings.

Caesar's Own Pizza

4-1/2 cups	all-purpose flour	1.125 L
2	pkg quick-rising (instant) dry yeast (or 2 tbsp/25 mL)	2
1/4 cup	finely chopped fresh basil (optional)	50 mL
2 tsp	salt	10 mL
1 tsp	granulated sugar	5 mL
1-3/4 cups	hot water	425 mL
3 tbsp	olive oil	50 mL
	Cornmeal	
1/3 cup	freshly grated Parmesan cheese	75 mL
	CAESAR TOPPING	
1/4 cup	light sour cream	50 mL
3 tbsp	water	50 mL
2 tbsp	light mayonnaise	25 mL
2 tsp	lemon juice	10 mL
1	clove garlic, minced	1
1 tsp	Dijon mustard	5 mL
Pinch	each salt and pepper	Pinch
10 cups	torn romaine lettuce	2.5 L
3	plum tomatoes, chopped	3

● In large bowl, combine 4 cups (1 L) of the flour, yeast, basil (if using), salt and sugar. Stir in hot water and 1 tbsp (15 mL) of the oil. Stir in enough of the remaining flour to make firm but soft dough. Turn out dough onto lightly floured surface; knead for 10 minutes or until smooth and elastic. Cover with tea towel; let rest for 15 minutes.

● Divide dough into 6 pieces; roll each into ball. On lightly floured surface, roll out each ball to 8-inch (20 cm) circle; fold 1/2 inch (1 cm) of edge toward center to form raised rim. Place 2 circles each onto three cornmeal-dusted baking sheets. Brush all over with remaining oil; sprinkle with 1/4 cup (50 mL) of the Parmesan cheese.

● Bake, one sheet at a time, in bottom third of 450°F (230°C) oven for 15 to 20 minutes or until golden brown and bottom is crisp.

● CAESAR TOPPING: Meanwhile, in large bowl, whisk together sour cream, water, mayonnaise, lemon juice, garlic, mustard, salt and pepper. Add lettuce and tomatoes; toss to coat. Heap onto each pizza crust. Sprinkle with remaining Parmesan cheese. Makes 6 pizzas.

N*o, there is no historical record of Caesar eating pizza — but if he did, we're sure this crisp and fresh romaine-and-tomato-salad-topped one would be his first choice!*

Per pizza: about
- 486 calories
- 12 g fat
- excellent source of iron
- 16 g protein
- 79 g carbohydrate
- high source of fiber

TIP: This dough is also sufficient for three 12-inch (30 cm) pizza crusts.

YOUR OWN PIZZERIA

Making pizza is as easy as pie, and you can top it with just about anything you like. Use the guidelines below, then let your own tastes and imagination go to work. Remember, too, that a pizza can be divided into four quadrants, each one slightly different for different people at your table.

● For a 12-inch (30 cm) round, enough for 2 adult dinner servings, you need about 2 cups (500 mL) shredded cheese, 1/2 to 3/4 cup (125 to 175 mL) tomato pizza or pasta sauce, and about 2 cups (500 mL) total toppings.

● For maximum distribution of flavors, moist juiciness and ease of serving, the pizza should be layered as follows: Spread base with sauce, sprinkle with half of the cheese, all of the toppings and then the rest of the cheese (this keeps the toppings from drying out).

● Bake topped pizzas on bottom rack of 500°F (260°C) oven for about 12 minutes, slightly more if crust is thick, slightly less if crust and toppings are thin.

Kid-Pleasing: Toppings include pepperoni, bacon, ham, smoked chicken or turkey and maybe sliced mushrooms, onions and green peppers. Ask first. Some kids just love olives.

Broccoli: Add blanched broccoli, bacon or ham and Cheddar cheese. Sweet red pepper rings provide color.

Chicken or Shrimp: Nestle sautéed chicken strips among toppings before baking. For shrimp, bake pizza for about 8 minutes without last layer of cheese. Sprinkle pizza with uncooked cleaned and shelled shrimp, then cheese. Return to oven for about 5 minutes. If using cooked cleaned salad shrimp, add at 10-minute mark with remaining cheese.

Smoked Salmon Pizza ▼

Other smoked fish — mackerel or trout, for example — are excellent on this crisp base with a creamy dill spread. Both are easy to skin, bone and break apart to set atop a wedge.

Per slice: about
• 146 calories   • 6 g protein
• 5 g fat   • 20 g carbohydrate

1	unbaked 12-inch (30 cm) pizza base (see Pizza Doughs, p. 73)	1
1 tbsp	light mayonnaise	15 mL
Half	small red onion, thinly sliced	Half
1/3 cup	light cream cheese	75 mL
1 tbsp	light sour cream	15 mL
1 tbsp	chopped fresh dill	15 mL
8	slices smoked salmon (4 oz/125 g)	8
8	fresh dill sprigs	8

● Spread pizza base with mayonnaise. Sprinkle with onion. Bake in bottom third of 500°F (260°C) oven for about 8 minutes or until crust is golden and slightly puffed.

● Meanwhile, in small bowl, mash cream cheese with sour cream; mix in dill. Drop by tablespoonfuls (15 mL) onto pizza; let stand for 30 seconds before spreading evenly over base. Cut into slices. Fold salmon slice over each slice; garnish with dill sprig. Makes 8 slices.

Apple Cinnamon Pizza ▼

Dessert pizza? Why not! Just remember to serve it fresh from the oven, when the flavors are at their best.

Per slice: about
• 163 calories   • 3 g protein
• 4 g fat   • 29 g carbohydrate

1	unbaked 12-inch (30 cm) pizza base (see Pizza Doughs, p. 73)	1
1/3 cup	dried cranberries or raisins (optional)	75 mL
3 cups	finely chopped peeled apples	750 mL
3 tbsp	granulated sugar	50 mL
2 tbsp	butter, melted	25 mL
1 tbsp	lemon juice	15 mL
1-1/2 tsp	cinnamon	7 mL

● Sprinkle pizza base with cranberries (if using). In bowl, toss together apples, sugar, butter, lemon juice and cinnamon; sprinkle over base.

● Bake in center of 450°F (230°C) oven for about 15 minutes or until crust is golden and slightly puffed and apples are tender. Let stand for 5 minutes; using scissors, cut into slices. Makes 8 slices.

Egg and Bacon Pizza ▼

1	unbaked 12-inch (30 cm) pizza base (see Pizza Doughs, p. 73)	1
2 tsp	Dijon mustard (optional)	10 mL
6	slices lean bacon	6
3/4 cup	sliced green onions	175 mL
4	eggs	4
Pinch	each pepper and nutmeg	Pinch
1-1/2 cups	shredded Oka cheese	375 mL

● Spread pizza base with mustard (if using). Bake in bottom third of 500°F (260°C) oven for about 5 minutes or until light brown; set aside.

● Meanwhile, in skillet, cook bacon over medium heat for 6 minutes or until crisp. Drain on paper towel; chop. Sprinkle over base along with onions.

● In bowl, whisk together eggs, pepper and nutmeg; pour over pizza. Sprinkle with cheese. Bake for 6 to 8 minutes or until crust is golden and puffed and eggs are set. Makes 8 slices.

Here's one pizza that's perfect for breakfast or as part of a pizza brunch.

Per slice: about
- 249 calories
- 13 g fat
- good source of calcium
- 14 g protein
- 19 g carbohydrate

TIP: Add half a sweet red pepper, chopped, along with onions if desired. If you can't find Oka cheese, use Gruyère, Swiss or Danbo.

Mushroom Squash Pizza ▼

Half	acorn squash, seeded	Half
2 tbsp	butter	25 mL
1	onion, chopped	1
3 cups	sliced mushrooms (8 oz/250 g)	750 mL
1/2 tsp	dried thyme	2 mL
1/4 tsp	dried sage	1 mL
Pinch	each salt and pepper	Pinch
2 tbsp	vegetable or chicken stock	25 mL
1	unbaked 12-inch (30 cm) pizza base (see Pizza Doughs, p. 73)	1
1-1/2 cups	shredded old Cheddar cheese	375 mL

● Place squash, cut side down, in small foil-lined pan; add 1/4 inch (5 mm) water. Bake in bottom third of 375°F (190°C) oven for about 30 minutes or until tender. Let cool; peel and cut into bite-size cubes to make 2 cups (500 mL).

● Meanwhile, in large heavy skillet, melt butter over medium heat; cook onion, stirring often, for about 8 minutes or until softened. Add mushrooms, thyme, sage, salt and pepper; cook, stirring often, for about 5 minutes or until softened and liquid is evaporated. Remove from heat; stir in stock. Add cubed squash, tossing gently to combine.

● Spoon mushroom mixture over pizza base; sprinkle with cheese. Bake in bottom third of 500°F (260°C) oven for about 10 minutes or until cheese is bubbly and crust is golden and slightly puffed. Makes 8 slices.

Although the combination of toppings may seem unusual, sage and thyme flavor and meld them into an irresistible autumn pizza.

Per slice: about
- 227 calories
- 11 g fat
- good source of calcium
- 9 g protein
- 23 g carbohydrate

(Left) A brunch assortment of Smoked Salmon, Egg and Bacon, Apple Cinnamon and Mushroom Squash pizza slices.

Quick Broccoli Whole Wheat Pizza ▶

Because the crust is leavened with baking powder and baking soda, this pizza is much quicker to make than most.

Per serving: about
- 400 calories
- 13 g fat
- very high source of fiber
- good source of iron
- 17 g protein
- 57 g carbohydrate
- excellent source of calcium

TIP: If Italian Spice stewed tomatoes are unavailable, substitute regular stewed tomatoes and 1/2 tsp (2 mL) dried basil.

1-1/2 cups	whole wheat flour	375 mL
1 cup	all-purpose flour	250 mL
1 cup	cornmeal	250 mL
2 tsp	baking powder	10 mL
1 tsp	baking soda	5 mL
1 tsp	salt	5 mL
1-1/2 cups	plain low-fat yogurt	375 mL
1/4 cup	canola oil	50 mL
	TOPPING	
2	cans (each 19 oz/540 mL) Italian Spice stewed tomatoes	2
2 cups	broccoli florets	500 mL
1 cup	thinly sliced carrots	250 mL
1-1/2 cups	shredded part-skim mozzarella cheese	375 mL
	Salt and pepper	
1	sweet green pepper, chopped	1
1/4 cup	freshly grated Parmesan cheese	50 mL

● In large bowl, stir together whole wheat and all-purpose flours, cornmeal, baking powder, baking soda and salt. Combine yogurt and oil; pour over flour mixture and stir with fork to combine.

● Turn out dough onto lightly floured surface; knead lightly into ball. With dampened hands, press into lightly greased 15- x 10-inch (40 x 25 cm) rimmed baking sheet. Bake in 400°F (200°C) oven for 10 to 12 minutes or until firm.

● TOPPING: Meanwhile, drain and chop tomatoes, reserving juice for other use; return tomatoes to sieve and set aside to let drain. In saucepan of boiling water, cook broccoli and carrots for 2 to 3 minutes or until partially cooked but still crunchy. Drain and refresh under cold water; drain well.

● Sprinkle half of the mozzarella over crust; spread tomatoes over top. Sprinkle with salt and pepper to taste. Top with broccoli, carrots, green pepper, remaining mozzarella and Parmesan cheese. Bake for 15 to 20 minutes or until bottom of crust is golden. Makes 8 servings.

Pizza Bianca

Pizza topped with fresh ricotta and tender, vibrantly green spinach is a delicious Italian tradition.

Per slice: about
- 224 calories
- 11 g fat
- good source of calcium
- 11 g protein
- 20 g carbohydrate

1	unbaked 12-inch (30 cm) pizza base (see Pizza Doughs, p. 73)	1
1 tbsp	olive oil	15 mL
1 cup	ricotta cheese	250 mL
1 tsp	chopped fresh rosemary or basil (optional)	5 mL
1/4 tsp	salt	1 mL
Pinch	nutmeg	Pinch
1/2 cup	chopped cooked spinach	125 mL
1 cup	shredded mozzarella cheese	250 mL
1/4 cup	freshly grated Parmesan cheese	50 mL

● Bake pizza base in bottom third of 500°F (260°C) oven for 5 minutes or until edge is lightly browned and crisp. Let cool. Brush with olive oil.

● In small bowl, combine ricotta cheese, rosemary (if using), salt and nutmeg; spread evenly over pizza base. Sprinkle with spinach, then mozzarella and Parmesan cheeses.

● Bake for 8 to 10 minutes or until topping is heated through, cheese melted and crust is golden and slightly puffed. Let stand for 5 minutes before cutting. Makes 8 slices.

Pesto Potato Pizza

This utterly delicious pizza is based on a bean/wheat flour dough that also makes a tasty bread or a focaccia.

Per serving: about
- 620 calories
- 22 g fat
- very high source of fiber
- 25 g protein
- 83 g carbohydrate
- excellent source of calcium and iron

TIP: If pesto is very thick, stir in up to 1 tbsp (15 mL) olive oil or water before spreading on dough.

1/3 cup	pesto	75 mL
4	cooked potatoes (peeled or unpeeled), thinly sliced	4
1/4 tsp	pepper	1 mL
2 cups	shredded Swiss cheese	500 mL
2	tomatoes, chopped	2
	BEAN BREAD DOUGH	
1 tbsp	granulated sugar	15 mL
1 cup	warm water	250 mL
2 tsp	active dry yeast	10 mL
1 cup	cooked or canned navy beans, drained and rinsed	250 mL
2 tbsp	vegetable oil	25 mL
2-1/4 cups	(approx) all-purpose flour	550 mL
1 cup	whole wheat flour	250 mL
1-1/2 tsp	salt	7 mL

● BEAN BREAD DOUGH: In large bowl, dissolve sugar in warm water. Sprinkle in yeast; let stand for 10 minutes or until frothy. Meanwhile, in food processor, purée beans with oil until smooth; add to yeast mixture. With electric mixer, beat in 1 cup (250 mL) of the all-purpose flour, whole wheat flour and salt; beat for 1 minute or until sticky dough forms. With wooden spoon, gradually stir in enough of the remaining flour to make stiff dough.

● Turn out dough onto lightly floured surface. Knead for about 8 minutes or until smooth and elastic, adding up to 1/4 cup (50 mL) more flour if necessary. Place in greased bowl, turning to grease all over. Cover with plastic wrap; let rise in warm draft-free place until doubled in bulk, 1 to 1-1/2 hours.

● Punch down dough; turn out onto lightly floured surface. Roll out into 17- x 11-inch (43 x 28 cm) rectangle; place on lightly greased baking sheet. Spread with pesto, leaving 1/2-inch (1 cm) border uncovered. Arrange potatoes in single layer over top. Sprinkle with pepper. Top with cheese and tomatoes.

● Bake in bottom third of 500°F (260°C) oven for about 15 minutes or until bottom is golden and crisp and cheese is melted. Makes 6 servings.

BEAN BREAD FOCACCIA

● Prepare Bean Bread Dough to end of first rise. Cut dough into 4 equal portions; roll out each into 1/2-inch (1 cm) thick circle. Sprinkle 1 tbsp (15 mL) cornmeal evenly over large rimmed baking sheets; place dough on top. Cover and let rise in warm draft-free place until doubled in bulk, about 30 minutes.

● Brush with 2 tbsp (25 mL) extra virgin olive oil; press fingers into top to make dimpled effect. Sprinkle with 1/4 tsp (1 mL) each salt and pepper. Bake in bottom third of 400°F (200°C) oven for about 20 minutes or until golden and focaccias sound hollow when tapped on bottom. Makes 4 servings.

Per serving: about • 570 calories • 16 g protein
• 15 g fat • 93 g carbohydrate • very high source of fiber
• excellent source of iron

POWER-PACKED BEAN BREAD

● Prepare Bean Bread Dough to end of first rise. Punch down dough; turn out onto lightly floured surface. Gently pull into 11- x 8-inch (28 x 20 cm) rectangle. Starting at one narrow end, roll up into tight cylinder; pinch along seam to smooth and seal. Place, seam side down, in greased 8- x 4-inch (1.5 L) loaf pan. Cover and let rise in warm draft-free place until doubled in bulk, about 1 hour.

● Brush top with 2 tsp (10 mL) milk. Bake in center of 400°F (200°C) oven for 30 minutes or until golden and loaf sounds hollow when tapped on bottom. Remove from pan; let cool on rack. Makes 1 loaf, 12 slices.

Per slice: about • 170 calories • 5 g protein • 3 g fat
• 30 g carbohydrate

Mushroom, Tomato and Chèvre Pizza

1	9-inch (23 cm) pita bread	1
1 tbsp	cream goat cheese (chèvre)	15 mL
3 tbsp	tomato sauce	50 mL
2	tomatoes, sliced	2
2	mushrooms, sliced	2
2 tsp	chopped fresh basil	10 mL
1/4 cup	shredded part-skim mozzarella cheese	50 mL
1 tsp	freshly grated Parmesan cheese	5 mL

● Place pita bread on baking sheet. Spread with goat cheese; top with tomato sauce. Cover with tomatoes and mushrooms; sprinkle with basil. Sprinkle with mozzarella and Parmesan cheeses.

● Bake in center of 475°F (240°C) oven for about 10 minutes or until cheese is bubbling and crust is browned. Makes 2 servings.

Tomatoes, mushrooms and goat cheese star in a shortcut pizza that uses pita bread instead of a regular pizza crust.

Per serving: about
- 290 calories
- 9 g fat
- good source of iron
- 17 g protein
- 38 g carbohydrate
- excellent source of calcium

TIP: A small prebaked pizza base is also a perfect vehicle for these healthy toppings. Bake a few minutes longer.

Pesto and Roasted Eggplant Pizza ▼

1	small eggplant (about 8 oz/250 g)	1
3 tbsp	olive oil	50 mL
1/4 tsp	each salt and pepper	1 mL
2/3 cup	prepared pesto	150 mL
1	unbaked 12-inch (30 cm) pizza base (see Pizza Doughs, p. 73)	1
1-1/2 cups	shredded Fontina or mozzarella cheese	375 mL
1/2 cup	diced plum tomatoes	125 mL

● Cut eggplant into 1/2-inch (1 cm) thick slices; cut each in half crosswise. Brush baking sheet with 2 tsp (10 mL) of the oil; arrange eggplant in single layer on top. Brush with 1 tbsp (15 mL) more of the oil; sprinkle with salt and pepper. Roast in 425°F (220°C) oven, turning halfway through, for about 30 minutes or until dark and tender.

● Spread 1/2 cup (125 mL) of the pesto over pizza base; sprinkle with Fontina cheese.

Arrange eggplant over top, then tomatoes. Combine remaining oil and pesto; drizzle over tomatoes.

● Bake in bottom third of 500°F (260°C) oven for 10 minutes or until cheese is bubbly and crust is golden and slightly puffed. Makes 8 slices.

TIP: If you can find slender Japanese eggplant, use two; slice on the diagonal and do not cut slices in half.

For the pizza lover with a taste for adventure — this one's for you!

Per slice: about
- 312 calories
- 21 g fat
- good source of calcium
- 10 g protein
- 21 g carbohydrate

ALMOST INSTANT PIZZAS

QUICKIE PIZZAS

These made-to-order pizzas make a great after-school snack or a quick meal with a salad on the side.

● For the base, use English muffins, split bagels or miniature pita breads. Spread the base with thick tomato sauce and sprinkle sparingly with dried oregano.
● Add your favorite toppings — a variety of shredded cheeses, diced cooked chicken or cooked sausage, sliced hotdogs, chopped sweet red or green peppers, tomato slices, drained pineapple chunks, diced green onions, sliced mushrooms.
● Broil just until toppings are heated through and cheese begins to bubble.

TOASTY PIZZA SANDWICHES

Get that sandwich maker busy for breakfast, lunch, snack or supper pizzawiches.

● Divide 1/4 cup (50 mL) pasta sauce among 4 slices whole wheat bread, spreading evenly over 1 side of each. Chop 2 slices capocollo or ham; sprinkle over 2 of the bread slices. Sprinkle with 1/4 cup (50 mL) diced mushrooms; top each with 1 slice mozzarella cheese, then remaining bread, sauce side down.
● Place in lightly greased sandwich maker and lock lid; cook for about 3 minutes or according to manufacturer's directions or until bread is toasted and cheese is melted. Let cool slightly. Makes 2 servings.

Per serving: about • 237 calories •
11 g protein • 8 g fat • 34 g carbohydrate
• very high source of fiber
• good source of calcium and iron

PIZZADILLAS

Pizza fillings are great on tortillas. These are perfect party fare for a casual gathering.

● Soak 12 dry-packed sun-dried tomato halves in boiling water for 15 minutes; drain and chop finely.
● Place six 7-inch (18 cm) flour tortillas on work surface; divide 1/4 cup (50 mL) shredded mozzarella cheese evenly over bottom half of each tortilla. Top with 1-1/3 cups (325 mL) thinly sliced mushrooms, tomatoes and 1/4 cup (50 mL) shredded fresh basil leaves. Sprinkle with additional 2-3/4 cups (675 mL) mozzarella cheese. Fold over. *(Pizzadillas can be prepared to this point, covered and refrigerated for up to 8 hours.)*
● Heat nonstick skillet over medium heat; cook stuffed tortillas, two at a time, for about 2 minutes per side or until filling is piping hot. (Or bake on baking sheet in 400°F/200°C oven for 8 minutes, turning halfway through.) Let stand for 5 minutes. Cut each into 3 wedges. Makes 18 pieces.

Per piece:
about
• 99 calories
• 5 g protein
• 5 g fat
• 8 g carbohydrate

SMILEY FREEZER PIZZA ▼

When there are busy days ahead, get ready with a pizza or two tucked in the freezer.

● Spread one (12-inch/30 cm) prebaked pizza crust with 1 cup (250 mL) chunky vegetable spaghetti sauce; sprinkle with 1 cup (250 mL) shredded mozzarella cheese and 1/4 cup (50 mL) freshly grated Parmesan cheese.
● Cut 2 oz (50 g) sliced ham and half a sweet green and/or red pepper into shapes for eyes, nose and mouth. Arrange over cheese along with 1/3 cup (75 mL) frozen green peas to make faces. Wrap and freeze pizza for up to 1 week.
● To heat, place frozen pizza on perforated pizza pan or baking sheet. Bake on bottom rack of 425°F (220°C) oven for about 15 minutes or until golden. Let stand for 5 minutes. Makes 4 servings.

Mediterranean Appetizer Squares

3	plum tomatoes, thinly sliced (8 oz/250 g)	3
1/3 cup	chopped black olives	75 mL
1 tbsp	chopped fresh basil (or 1 tsp/5 mL dried)	15 mL
1/4 tsp	pepper	1 mL
2 tsp	olive oil	10 mL
1-1/2 cups	shredded Monterey Jack cheese	375 mL
	CRUST	
1/4 cup	cornmeal	50 mL
1-3/4 cups	all-purpose flour	425 mL
1 tbsp	baking powder	15 mL
1 tsp	salt	5 mL
1/3 cup	cold shortening	75 mL
3/4 cup	milk	175 mL

● CRUST: Sprinkle 15- x 10-inch (40 x 25 cm) rimmed baking sheet with 1 tsp (5 mL) of the cornmeal; set aside.

● In bowl, combine remaining cornmeal, flour, baking powder and salt; with pastry blender or two knives, cut in shortening until in coarse crumbs. Add milk all at once, stirring with fork to make soft, slightly sticky dough. Turn out onto lightly floured surface; knead 10 times. Roll out into rectangle to fit pan.

● Arrange tomatoes over crust; sprinkle with olives, basil and pepper. Drizzle with oil; sprinkle with cheese. Bake in bottom third of 425°F (220°C) oven for about 15 minutes or until cheese is bubbly and crust is browned. Slide off pan onto rack; let cool for 5 minutes. Transfer to cutting board; cut into squares. Makes 30 pieces.

A large pizza made with a quick biscuit base is an excellent appetizer for summer barbecues. It's also a fine contribution to a class party or bake sale.

Per piece: about
- 81 calories
- 5 g fat
- 3 g protein
- 7 g carbohydrate

Pizza Pot Pie

1 tsp	olive oil	5 mL
1	each onion and sweet green pepper, chopped	1
2	cloves garlic, minced	2
2 tsp	chili powder	10 mL
1 tsp	ground cumin	5 mL
8 oz	lean ground beef	250 g
8 oz	chorizo sausage, sliced	250 g
1 cup	frozen corn kernels	250 mL
1-1/2 cups	salsa	375 mL
1 tbsp	dried oregano	15 mL
2 cups	shredded light Cheddar-style cheese	500 mL
1 lb	pizza dough	500 g
2 tbsp	freshly grated Parmesan cheese	25 mL

● In nonstick skillet, heat oil over medium heat; cook onion, green pepper, garlic, chili powder and cumin, stirring occasionally, for 5 minutes. Add beef; cook, breaking up meat with wooden spoon, for 5 minutes or until no longer pink.

● Remove from heat; mix in sausage, corn, salsa and 2 tsp (10 mL) of the oregano. Pour into 13- x 9-inch (3 L) baking dish. Sprinkle with Cheddar cheese.

● On lightly floured surface, roll out dough 1 inch (2.5 cm) larger than dish; place over filling, tucking in excess. Sprinkle with Parmesan and remaining oregano. Bake in 400°F (200°C) oven for 30 minutes or until golden and filling is bubbly. Let stand for 10 minutes. Makes 4 servings.

S ausages are a quick and easy way to get a whole lot of flavor in this pizza-inspired pie. Look for tender, freshly made Portuguese or Spanish chorizo or Italian sausage.

Per serving: about
- 965 calories
- 49 g fat
- very high source of fiber
- 54 g protein
- 77 g carbohydrate
- excellent source of calcium and iron

TIP: Use bought pizza dough or, following method for Food Processor or Handmade Dough (p. 73), make 1 lb (500 g) dough using 2/3 cup (150 mL) water, 2 tsp (10 mL) olive oil, 2 cups (500 mL) all-purpose flour, 1-1/2 tsp (7 mL) quick-rising (instant) dry yeast and 1/2 tsp (2 mL) salt.

Deep-Dish Vegetable Pizza

Pizza does look like a pie when it's baked in a deep dish. Each wedge contains healthy broccoli, savory onions, mushrooms and red pepper plus a topping of Asiago cheese.

Per serving: about
- 384 calories
- 13 g protein
- 15 g fat
- 50 g carbohydrate
- good source of calcium

1 tbsp	vegetable oil	15 mL
1 cup	thinly sliced onions	250 mL
2	cloves garlic, minced	2
1 cup	sliced mushrooms	250 mL
1	sweet red pepper, thinly sliced	1
1/4 tsp	each salt and pepper	1 mL
1 cup	shredded Asiago cheese	250 mL
1 cup	broccoli florets	250 mL
1	batch Handmade Pizza Dough (p. 73)	1
	Cornmeal	
1/2 cup	pizza sauce	125 mL
1 tbsp	chopped fresh basil	15 mL

● In skillet, heat oil over medium-high heat; cook onion and garlic, stirring occasionally, for about 5 minutes or until softened. Add mushrooms and red pepper; cook, stirring occasionally, for about 6 minutes or until liquid is evaporated and vegetables start to brown. Stir in salt, pepper and half of the Asiago cheese.

● Meanwhile, in large pot of boiling salted water, cook broccoli for about 2 minutes or until tender-crisp. Drain and refresh under cold water; drain well.

● Roll out pizza dough into 11-inch (28 cm) circle; fit into cornmeal-dusted 9-inch (1.5 L) round cake pan or pie plate, pressing up side to rim. Combine pizza sauce and basil; spread over dough. Cover with broccoli, then mushroom mixture. Sprinkle evenly with remaining cheese. Bake in bottom third of 500°F (260°C) oven for about 20 minutes or until crust is golden and topping is bubbly. Makes 4 servings.

Ricotta and Pesto Calzone

When Robert Martella and Lucia Ruggiero Martella opened Grano in mid-town Toronto in 1986, these glossy half-moon turnovers were an instant hit. Here, they come sized for appetizers.

Per calzone: about
- 377 calories
- 14 g protein
- 19 g fat
- 36 g carbohydrate
- good source of calcium and iron

1	pkg active dry yeast (or 1 tbsp/15 mL)	1
2 cups	warm water	500 mL
1/4 cup	olive oil	50 mL
1 tsp	salt	5 mL
4-1/4 cups	(approx) all-purpose flour	1.125 L
	FILLING	
4	eggs	4
1 lb	ricotta cheese	500 g
2/3 cup	pesto	150 mL
1/2 cup	freshly grated Parmesan cheese	125 mL
1/2 tsp	salt	2 mL
1 tbsp	olive oil	15 mL
1 tsp	dried oregano	5 mL

● In large bowl, sprinkle yeast in warm water; let stand for 10 minutes or until frothy. Blend in half of the oil and the salt. With electric mixer, beat in half of the flour.

● Turn out dough onto lightly floured surface; knead for about 10 minutes or until smooth and elastic, adding enough of the remaining flour as necessary. Cover with tea towel; let rest in warm draft-free place for 15 minutes.

● Grease 3 rimmed baking sheets with remaining oil. Divide dough into 12 portions; form each into ball. Place on prepared baking sheets. Cover and let rise in warm draft-free place until tripled in bulk, 30 to 40 minutes. Using fingertips, press each portion into 5-inch (12 cm) circle.

● FILLING: In bowl, mix together eggs, ricotta, pesto, Parmesan and salt. Divide among dough rounds; fold dough over to make half-circles, leaving enough dough on bottom edge to fold over top edge. Pinch or crimp edges to seal attractively. Bake in 375°F (190°C) oven for 20 minutes or until golden. Brush with oil; sprinkle with oregano. Makes 12 small calzone.

Kangaroos

2 tbsp	buttermilk	25 mL
	CRUST	
1 tsp	active dry yeast	5 mL
1 tbsp	warm water	15 mL
1-2/3 cups	all-purpose flour	400 mL
1 tbsp	granulated sugar	15 mL
1 tsp	baking powder	5 mL
1/2 tsp	baking soda	2 mL
1/2 tsp	salt	2 mL
2 tbsp	butter	25 mL
3/4 cup	(approx) buttermilk	175 mL
	PIZZA FILLING	
12 oz	lean ground beef	375 g
1 cup	pizza sauce	250 mL
1 tsp	dried oregano	5 mL
1/2 tsp	pepper	2 mL
Pinch	salt	Pinch
1 cup	shredded part-skim mozzarella cheese	250 mL

● PIZZA FILLING: In nonstick skillet, brown beef over medium heat, breaking up with spoon. Drain off fat. Stir in pizza sauce, oregano, pepper and salt. Let cool.

● CRUST: In small bowl, sprinkle yeast in warm water; let stand for 10 minutes or until frothy. In large bowl, stir together flour, sugar, baking powder, baking soda and salt; with pastry blender or two knives, cut in butter until mixture is crumbly. Stir in yeast mixture and 3/4 cup (175 mL) buttermilk.

● Turn out dough onto lightly floured surface; knead just until dough holds together. Divide into 8 pieces; roll out each into 6-inch (15 cm) circle. Place 2 heaping tablespoonfuls (25 mL) of filling on half of each circle; sprinkle with 2 tbsp (25 mL) mozzarella. Moisten edges of dough with water; fold dough over to make half-moon shapes, pressing edges firmly with fork to seal.

● Brush tops with buttermilk. Place on ungreased baking sheet; bake in 350°F (180°C) oven for 15 to 20 minutes or until golden brown. Makes 8 servings.

VARIATION

● CURRY FILLING: In nonstick skillet, brown 8 oz (250 g) ground turkey, chicken or beef over medium heat. Stir in 1/2 cup (125 mL) each diced onion, diced potato and frozen peas, 1/2 cup (125 mL) water, 1 tbsp (15 mL) curry powder, and salt and pepper to taste. Reduce heat to medium-low; cook for 12 to 15 minutes or until vegetables are tender. Stir in 2 tbsp (25 mL) chutney. Let cool.

So kangaroos have pockets, and pockets in these nifty turnovers contain a pizza filling that's sure to please kids for snacks, lunches and suppers. Mabel Wong of Yellowknife, N.W.T., sent us this recipe to celebrate Canadian Living's 20th anniversary.

Per serving: about
- 280 calories
- 16 g protein
- 11 g fat
- 29 g carbohydrate
- good source of calcium and iron

PIZZA PANS

● Readily available metal pizza pans are just fine for pizzas. Choose the heaviest, shiniest ones you can find. Just remember to bake pizza on the bottom rack of the oven so that the blast of heat from below sets the bottom of the crust.

● Perforated pizza pans are also acceptable but, in our experience, not better than a heavy round pizza pan.

● When there are many mouths to feed, use rimmed baking sheets in a size that fits your crowd.

● Pizza stones are a fine alternative to pans, and preferred among pizza cognoscente. Preheat according to the manufacturer's instructions and you will have a crisp-bottomed and pizzeria-like pizza.

Italian Sausage Calzone

Calzone make ideal lunches, either to carry and heat up, or at home.

Per serving: about
- 702 calories
- 26 g fat
- excellent source of iron and calcium
- 30 g protein
- 87 g carbohydrate
- high source of fiber

2 tsp	vegetable oil	10 mL
1	onion, thinly sliced	1
2	cloves garlic, minced	2
1/2 tsp	dried Italian herb seasoning	2 mL
1	sweet green pepper, thinly sliced	1
1-1/2 cups	sliced mushrooms	375 mL
2	Italian sausages	2
3/4 cup	pasta sauce	175 mL
2	batches Handmade Pizza Dough (p. 73)	2
1-1/4 cups	shredded mozzarella cheese	300 mL
1/4 cup	freshly grated Parmesan cheese	50 mL

● In large nonstick skillet, heat oil over medium-high heat; cook onion, garlic and Italian herb seasoning for 3 minutes or until softened. Add green pepper and mushrooms; cook for 8 minutes or until browning and liquid is evaporated; transfer to bowl.

● Remove sausages from casings. Crumble sausage into skillet; cook, breaking up with back of spoon, for about 5 minutes or until browned. Drain off fat. Stir in pasta sauce and vegetables; cook for 3 minutes. Set aside.

● On lightly floured surface, divide each batch of dough in half to make 4 portions. Roll out each portion into 8-inch (20 cm) circle. Divide sausage filling evenly over one-half of each round, leaving 1-1/2-inch (4 cm) border uncovered at edge.

● Combine mozzarella and Parmesan cheeses; sprinkle evenly over each filling. Fold dough over filling and fold edges over together; press firmly to seal. Transfer to lightly greased baking sheet; prick tops several times with tip of sharp knife.

● Bake in center of 400°F (200°C) oven for 25 minutes or until heated through and golden brown. Let stand for 15 minutes before serving. Makes 4 servings.

TIP: Here's how to buy what you need for calzone or pizzas. Each 4 oz (125 g) mushrooms yields 1-1/2 cups (375 mL) sliced. For 1 cup (250 mL) shredded mozzarella or other similar cheese, you'll need 4 oz (125 g); for grated Parmesan, you'll need about 1/2 oz (15 g) more. One average jar pasta sauce yields almost 3 cups (750 mL).

Braided Pizza Sandwich ▶

All the pizza ingredients are the same — tomatoes, ground beef, oregano, cheese and pizza dough — but the presentation is spectacular when you braid the dough around this hearty filling.

Per serving: about
- 420 calories
- 17 g fat
- excellent source of iron
- 21 g protein
- 46 g carbohydrate

1 lb	pizza dough	500 g	1/2 tsp	pepper	2 mL
2 tbsp	cornmeal	25 mL	1 cup	diced zucchini	250 mL
1	egg, beaten	1	12 oz	lean ground beef	375 g
			1	can (19 oz/540 mL) tomatoes	1
	FILLING				
1 tsp	vegetable oil	5 mL	2 tsp	lemon juice	10 mL
1 cup	diced peeled eggplant	250 mL	1/2 cup	shredded Asiago or Swiss cheese	125 mL
1	onion, chopped	1			
2	cloves garlic, minced	2			
1-1/2 tsp	dried oregano	7 mL			
1 tsp	salt	5 mL			

● FILLING: In large skillet, heat oil over medium heat; cook eggplant, onion, garlic, oregano, salt and pepper, stirring frequently, for about 5 minutes or until softened.

● Add zucchini and beef, breaking up beef with back of spoon; cook for about 10 minutes or until beef is no longer pink. Skim off fat.

● Meanwhile, drain tomatoes, reserving juice for another use; coarsely chop tomatoes and add to pan along with lemon juice. Bring to boil; boil for about 2 minutes or until most of the liquid is evaporated. Let cool.

● On lightly floured surface, roll out pizza dough into 15- x 10-inch (38 x 25 cm) rectangle. Sprinkle cornmeal onto large baking sheet; transfer dough to sheet. Sprinkle cheese in 4-inch (10 cm) wide strip lengthwise down center of dough. Spoon meat mixture over cheese.

● Using sharp knife and starting at one corner of dough, make 10 cuts diagonally to form strips about 1-1/2 inches (4 cm) apart, stopping

about 1/2 inch (1 cm) before filling. Repeat with other side, starting at corner across from initial starting point. Fold first strip over filling; brush with some of the egg. Fold opposite strip over top. Repeat with remaining strips and egg to create braid.

● Bake in 425°F (220°C) oven for 5 minutes. Reduce temperature to 400°F (200°C); cook for about 15 minutes or until light golden brown on top. Makes 6 servings.

Bread-Making Basics

*The staff of life doesn't take a miracle to make. When you know how to knead
(mix and work) the dough properly, great loaves are guaranteed.*

1. Making the dough

Letting the yeast swell and froth in water is called proofing. If there is no increase in size or no presence of bubbles and foam, begin again with freshly purchased yeast that is within its best-before date.

● The sugar in the water nourishes and helps to activate the yeast while it softens. While a regular dinner or sandwich bread should not be sweet, the small amount of sugar called for in recipes — usually 1 tsp (5 mL) — is not enough to make the bread taste sweet.

● Water for active dry yeast should be slightly warmer than lukewarm, about 110°F (45°C). To test, a sprinkle on your wrist should register as slightly warm.

● Quick-rising (instant) dry yeast is made up of fine granules and is usually mixed directly into the flour and other dry ingredients. The temperature of the added liquid is usually higher than for active dry yeast, warmer but still comfortable to the touch, 120°F to 130°F (50°C to 55°C).

● Do not play around with the amount of salt in a recipe. Salt plays a key role in regulating the yeast and is necessary for the taste of bread.

● Place the proofing yeast in a warm place.

● It is prudent not to add all the flour called for before kneading. Hold back about 1/4 cup (50 mL) from total amount as it is easy to knead in more if the dough is too sticky.

● Using an electric mixer to add some of the flour speeds up the dough-making process. If you have a heavy-duty mixer, use the paddle attachment, changing to a dough hook when dough becomes stiff.

2. Kneading the dough

Kneading takes anywhere from 8 to 12 minutes. It's simply pulling the far side of the dough up and folding it over toward you, then pressing and pushing the dough away from you with the heels of your hands in a rolling motion. Give the dough a quarter turn before repeating the same motions and setting a rhythm that's both relaxing and vigorous. A well-kneaded dough is elastic. Try pressing with your fingertip and see it spring back.

● Most doughs can be kneaded in the food processor, although you may need to break your dough into batches to accommodate more than 3 cups (750 mL) flour. In a food processor, it takes about 1 minute to knead; in a heavy-duty mixer with dough hook, count on about half the required time to hand-knead the dough.

● Be sure to knead long enough for the dough to become smooth and elastic. Resist the temptation to add generous sprinkles of flour early on to prevent sticking as this can result in a dry bread. Instead, keep kneading, adding just a whisp of flour as absolutely necessary, because as the dough becomes stretchier, it absorbs some of its own moisture and naturally becomes less sticky.

● Note that dough containing rye flour, rolled oats or whole wheat flour is stickier than all-purpose flour dough and will absorb more flour. Some bread makers knead these doughs in a large bowl.

3. Letting dough rise and punching it down

The best place to let dough rise is in a large bowl. To prevent a skin from forming on the surface of the dough, grease the bowl using shortening, oil or your choice of fat, then add the dough and turn it to grease all over.

● The best cover for the bowl is plastic wrap, which holds in moisture. Choose a warm draft-free place, about 75°F (24°C), to let dough rise. A turned-off warm oven or a spot near a heat register or radiator is ideal. It usually takes from 1 to 3 hours for dough to double in bulk. Doughs rich in butter or other fat and eggs take longer to rise.

● Gently punch down dough to press out air. Very gently pull dough from side of bowl, turn dough over and form into a ball. Since your dough will be elastic from this brief handling, cover it with a tea towel and let it relax for 10 minutes. Now your dough is ready for shaping.

4. Shaping

If the dough becomes elastic during the shaping and resists rolling or forming, cover and let it rest for a few minutes before continuing.

● Depending on the amount of dough, form into one or two loaves or into 12 to 14 rolls or other sizes and shapes according to individual recipes.

● To form a loaf, gently pull dough into rectangle, one side about as long as the bread pan, the other dimension slightly longer. Starting at narrow side, roll firmly into cylinder. Pinch seam and ends firmly and place, seam side down, in greased pan.

● Shiny, heavy bread pans are preferred; dark nonstick pans give a darker crust and nonstick finishes may fail if scratched and worn. Grease pans with shortening or oil.

● Cover loaf with clean dry tea towel and set in warm draft-free place to rise until doubled in bulk again. This usually takes less time than the first rise. Gently press a finger 1/2 inch (1 cm) into risen dough; if the dent stays, the dough is ready to bake.

5. Glazing and baking

To glaze a loaf, brush dough with milk, a beaten egg, an egg white, or an egg yolk beaten with a spoonful of water or milk.

● Bake bread in the center of a preheated oven.

Temperatures and times will vary depending on the bread.

● It is always best to bake one pan of rolls at a time in the center of the oven. But, if pressed, set racks just below and just above the center slot and bake two pans at a time, switching and rotating pans halfway through.

● To test for doneness, invert loaf into tea towel and tap gently on bottom. The loaf should sound hollow. An instant-read thermometer is a sure guarantee of doneness; insert into center of bread. A loaf is ready if the thermometer registers 200°F (100°C). If the loaf is not yet done and the sides are still soft, return loaf to pan and bake for about 5 minutes longer before repeating test.

● To crisp a loaf all over, or if sides of loaf are firm but loaf is not quite done, remove loaf from pan and bake for 3 to 6 minutes longer on rack.

● Always remove bread from the pan immediately so steam doesn't develop between the crust and pan. The exception to this rule is a rich bread such as panettone that needs to cool in its pan so it won't collapse.

● Cool loaves, on their sides if loaves are tall, on a rack.

● Always cool bread fully before enclosing in paper or plastic bag to store or freeze. Homemade bread doesn't have any preservatives so plan on eating it within 3 days, depending on the bread and conditions.

The Contributors

For your easy reference, we have included an alphabetical listing of recipes by contributor.

Photography Credits

FRED BIRD:
pages 8, 16, 44, 47, 56, 60, 66, 79.

DOUGLAS BRADSHAW:
pages 3 (bottom), 7, 22, 63, 82.

CHRISTOPHER CAMPBELL:
pages 88 and 89.

ED O'NEILL:
page 15.

JOY VON TIEDEMANN:
page 76.

MICHAEL WARING:
pages 28, 30.

ROBERT WIGINGTON:
front cover; pages 3 (top and middle), 4, 11, 13, 19, 25, 27, 35, 37, 41, 50, 55, 57, 59, 69, 71, 72, 81, 87.

In the Canadian Living Test Kitchen. Clockwise from left: Elizabeth Baird (food director), Heather Howe (manager), Susan Van Hezewijk, Emily Richards, Donna Bartolini (associate food director), Daphna Rabinovitch (associate food director) and Jennifer MacKenzie.

Special Thanks

Praise and thanks go to the talented and enthusiastic team who put together *Canadian Living's Best Breads & Pizzas*. Baker extraordinaire and associate food director Donna Bartolini is responsible for the new breads created in the Canadian Living Test Kitchen especially for *Breads & Pizzas*. She was assisted by Test Kitchen home economists Emily Richards, Susan Van Hezewijk, Jennifer MacKenzie and manager Heather Howe. Appreciation goes also to associate food director Daphna Rabinovitch, our valued food writers (see p. 90), managing editor Susan Antonacci, editorial assistant Olga Goncalves, senior editor Julia Armstrong, our copy department under Michael Killingsworth and art department guided by Cate Cochran. Special thanks to our meticulous senior food editor, Beverley Renahan, for her high standards of consistency and accuracy. Thanks also for the support of editor-in-chief Bonnie Cowan and publisher Caren King.

There are others to thank, too. On the visual side — our photographers (noted above), plus prop stylists Maggi Jones, Janet Walkinshaw, Shelly Tauber, Bridget Sargeant and Susan Doherty-Hannaford who provide backgrounds, dishes and embellishments for the luscious food photos, and food stylists Kate Bush, Ruth Gangbar, Debby Charendoff Moses, Lucie Richard, Olga Truchan, Jennifer McLagan, Jill Snider, Sharon Dale and Kathy Robertson who do the creative baking and garnishing.

Book designers Gord Sibley and Dale Vokey are responsible for the splendid design of the Best Series. Thanks go to Albert Cummings, president of Madison Press Books.

Working with Wanda Nowakowska, associate editorial director of Madison Press, is always a pleasure, certainly for her high standard of workmanship and creativity, but also for her calm and always thoughtful nature. Thanks also to Tina Gaudino, Rosemary Hillary, Donna Chong of the production department and others at Madison Press. Appreciation for their contribution at Random House is extended to Duncan Shields, mass marketing sales manager; Mary Jane Boreham; members of the marketing and publicity departments — Kathleen Bain, Pat Cairns, Sheila Kay, Cathy Paine, Maria Medeiros, Deborah Bjorgan; and president and publisher David Kent.

Elizabeth Baird

Index

Over *ver 100 delicious homemade breads, bagels, baguettes, flatbreads, pizzas...and more*

CANADIAN LIVING
TESTED TILL PERFECT
KITCHEN

Trust Canadian Living to bring you the BEST!

Watch for more new books in the months ahead.